MW00581291

EASTERN STAR RISING

EASTERN STAR RISING

How Satan's Eye of the Storm Was Created

LuciaBelia

Satan's Eye Of The Storm LLC

Eastern Star Rising: How Satan's Eye of the Storm Was Created

Published by Satan's Eye Of The Storm LLC

Library of Congress Control Number: 2023943038

ISBN (hardcover): 9781662940880
ISBN (paperback): 9781662940897
eISBN: 9781662940903

To E.A. Koetting, my mentor, teacher and humble Dark Master of the Black Flame burning within. This book would not be possible without his guidance and wisdom throughout my ascension. The three most valuable things I take with me are: Closing my eyes and connecting people with blue lights of energy. Not caring what anyone thinks about me. Lastly, giving 100% to what I do and giving back to others with genuine love and respect while doing it. I will always remember that I am the conduit that connects the storm of change and the storm of chaos or calm. Thank you E.A., you brought me Death in Abaddon's Abbyss and you showed me to the other side into Rebirth.

Table of Contents

Chapter 1
The Star Is Created

I am a convicted felon. I do not agree with my conviction; during the serving of my sentence, I filed an appeal. I lost my appeal on a 2-1 decision and I decided to serve my sentence with all the dignity I could muster. I made a choice to serve my time and not allow my time to serve me.

I was given the opportunity to serve in a therapeutic community for my five-year sentence. Looking back, I know Satan was looking out for me, telling me to make the most of this situation and to make changes within myself while I had opportunity, facilitators, and time.

It was during this time that I did shadow work, anger management using the Narcotics Anonymous 12 steps, and deep trauma work. It did not matter that I felt innocent on this charge. The only thing that mattered was that I was convicted, and my life was changing. I needed to be ok with it; I needed to learn to find my voice and adjust to this new life. I needed to be ok with what had happened, and I needed to not be a victim— but to instead figure out how to make this a lesson from which I could learn.

I am not going to give the details of what happened, because the person who accused me has profited enough from the story. We have all hit rock bottom in our lives at one point or another.

We need to figure out how to get back up, dust ourselves off, and stop allowing others to keep us down. We do not get to reinvent ourselves, per se, but we certainly do get to serve our time. We learn our lessons, whether deserved or not; we all get to move on, whether other people want us to or not.

I believe in life we hit crossroads and we keep re-looping these crossroads until we learn the lesson the demons want us to learn. I say I do not resist, but until I followed the left-hand path, I hit a few re-loops on the same crossroads, for sure.

This is my story. This is my journey on the left-hand path; this is how Satan and the Gatekeepers had me rise to mastery in six months, with the help of a few masters.

My decision to follow the left-hand path was not an accident. Looking back, I had been traveling on it—a long hard journey—since childhood. This is my story, and now, I realize it's my destiny.

I am an emissary of Satan not by accident, but by destiny.

"Our trajectory into the path is of our making, and we can resist it, or we can ride the star smoothly." So sayeth Satan, for each of us is a God, each of us is an entity of our own right, if we so choose. The answers we so valiantly and avidly seek are within us; if we only seek, we shall indeed find.

Those of us who create our magic as an extension of ourselves find success because the key is Demonic Magick. Those who continue to try to cast Demonic Magick continue to be its victim because they believe they must protect themselves from the things which they summon, never genuinely believing in what they do—therefore, never believing in themselves.

Demonic Magick is a calling, and you must decide to call, to answer, and to become.

***

Growing up in an Irish-Catholic home the fourth of five children and the favorite of my birth father was not an easy task. I was the youngest girl, and I was born with this gift. I was hated by my siblings and my mother. For decades, I did not understand why. When I was four years old, my oldest brother, whom I will not name, took me to the public park to play at my father's request days before my fifth birthday. He was seven years older than me, and he was told to play with me and make sure I didn't run off. But he wanted to play chess, so I was abandoned at the park. The rest is how history was created.

Feeling petulant, I decided I could fly—an effort to get attention—as you do at that age. Playing Wonder Woman, I jumped fifteen feet from an old-fashioned slide. I broke my collarbone and dislocated my shoulder blade. I was rushed home by the park ranger and a distraught and angry brother to an even angrier father who whisked me to the hospital. He was a chemist in a laboratory there, so I was given immediate care and lavished with attention because my dad, aka "Teddy" as all Irish were given nicknames, was adored.

My dad and I shared a birthday. In fact, I was the third generation of the family born at the same hour, on the same day, forty years apart. My birthday was spent that year in a harness brace. I was athletic and normally played outdoors all day long but because of my injury, I was confined to the couch.

My sister, who was two years older than me, had the displeasure of getting measles during my birthday confinement. My mom, totally absent while my dad was still around, was a labor and delivery room RN and had asked my older brother to bring my sister some Tylenol. There were two bottles, the almost-empty one he was distributing, and the brand-new one left on the counter with 500 flavored, chewable tablets. I was an inquisitive kid, so I asked my oldest brother what that bottle was. I was told that it was candy, and not to take any—they were for my sister only. It was my birthday; I was reckless and spoiled. I was five years old . . . do the math. No one was around so I did exactly what he wanted me to do. I took that 500-Tylenol-tablet bottle, hid behind the recliner, and ate all of it gleefully with wild abandon.

I was found two hours later, unconscious. I remember this as clearly as if it were yesterday: screaming, chaos, my mom, the registered nurse. I lost so much respect for her that day honestly, at five years old, while hovering over my body with two men next to me watching this unfold. I was so confused as to what the commotion was about. My brother was smirking but scared. My dad lifted me up, sobbing while doing CPR, as my red sneaker fell off my left foot.

A man I had never seen before stooped and picked it up calmly. I do not believe anyone noticed him there. He had the most beautiful blue eyes ever. I noticed because my piercing grey-blue eyes, same as my dad's, had always been commented on by friends and strangers alike. He looked me directly in the eyes up above the scene and placed his finger to his lips. He walked behind my dad to the station wagon while my mom drove to EMMC.

At EMMC, we were met yet again by an emergency team at the door with a stretcher. The team began CPR. I was rushed to a trauma room, not breathing. A nasogastric tube was shoved down my nose and activated charcoal was pumped into my stomach as compressions continued. To this day, I cannot have anything put into my nose. Even after hypnosis, I gag, choke, and hyperventilate.

The man next to my dad asked, "Teddy, what would you give to have her survive?"

His response was instant, "Everything and anything you ask and want. She is the reason I am sober."

I never knew my dad was a dry drunk. He was everything to us kids. He took us fishing, he fed us, he loved us . . . every memory from birth was of our dad caring for us. Every childhood photo was of me in my dad's arms, on his shoulders, or holding his hands. Sadly, I have no photos of my mom, no memory of my mom taking care of me, before I was seven years old.

The love I am capable of, the healing I can give to others, and what got me through the years of abuse growing up after my birth father left, was based on the first six years of love given to me by this man, my father. I owe him everything. Without him, I, of course, would not be born; but without him, I would not be alive either. He gave up everything he held dear to keep me and my petulant childhood alive. That is a gift I will never forget.

When I start to revert to fear-based living or selfish behavioral patterns, I stop and reflect on my father and think about what he sacrificed for me. All he did, so that I may live. It is a humbling experience. He lived alone the rest of his life, and I will forever in my heart be grateful and believe that when you love—genuinely love—the sacrifice you make is never a sacrifice, it is unconditional, eternal.

I looked at the two men beside me and asked what was happening. They smiled at me and said, "Go on, your dad just sacrificed everything he loves for you to live. Go back into yourself, it will not hurt, we promise. We will see you again for we will always be a part of you. You are a part of us and one day you will be back with us, as will your dad."

Confused, but understanding enough, I did as I was told. I closed my eyes and rejoined the scene down below with an understanding beyond my years.

I survived the overdose of 500 Tylenol with absolutely no consequences. Do not ask me how, because it should have destroyed my liver. I should have had some brain damage. At five years old, I was underweight—all of thirty-five pounds. I was a ballerina and a figure skater, and I fought to keep weight on. Every one of my siblings was stocky, except for me. I had my dad's slight frame.

I was the only child with grey-blue eyes and mine were the only ones that changed color with my temper from bright grey to cornflower blue. I was born with psychic abilities, like my dad, and his mom before him. I understood from birth things many did not. I had a maturity about me. I did not comprehend many thoughts I had, which were not appropriate knowledge. I spoke at an early age of things I had no business knowing. It took years for me to learn my knowledge was not always needed and understand that it was wise to hold my own counsel. However, in that moment of awakening from unconsciousness, I knew my life was forever changed and my grey-blue eyes never saw innocence again.

***

I had a best friend while growing up in my hometown. Starting from when we were six years old, we often drew pentagrams on the road. We cast spells and made potions with everything from basic bathroom cleaning supplies to my mom's kitchen herbs and spices. Anything that spoke to my heart was put in the bucket. Protection, evil castings to repay siblings, others who had needed retribution, and love incantations: I wrote them in a notebook I called: "XXX private keep out."

My dad found it, laughed, and said, "My love, keep this forever and one day you will look back and realize what you have."

I did not. I am not one to hold on to things or cherish anything materialistic. Unfortunately, I throw things away too quickly; my rule of thumb being if I have not used it in a year, I must dispose of it. I realize, looking back, that was my first grimoire, so I deeply regret no longer having it.

Chapter 2
The Ending That Marked the Beginning

My dad left in September 1975, a year after my overdose. All five of us kids watched him pack his briefcase for work with underwear and some clothes. We were curious; it was out of the norm. I remember crying because I knew he was gone.

My oldest brother chased after my dad and asked if he could go fishing with him before work. Our dad cast his rod every chance he got. My dad loaded his canoe and calmly told him, "No son, not today." My twelve-year-old brother burst into tears, begging my dad to take him wherever he was going. He chased the station wagon down the road.

As we saw it disappear into the distance, we all started to sob because we knew our dad was never coming home. I sat next to the lilac bush and talked to the beautiful, yellow-eyed man with the dragon's head for hours, asking why my dad had to go. My mom came home from work to find the other four distraught. I was still talking to the dragon's head calmly by myself. I think she thought I was delirious.

The dragon's head told me that my dad had to go so he would not kill my mom; that he had a drinking problem and was only staying sober for us children; and that he had made a deal with Satan for my life. In exchange, my dad was going to do things to improve himself. I did not really comprehend at the time, but I knew it was a done deal. I knew crying about it was a waste of time and my dad had to do this journey. In my "knowing," I realized I had to let go, and it was ok.

I was disappointed that my dad left me behind because he left me with my mom and siblings, knowing that they hated me. It was the start of my biggest fears: abandonment and distrust of love. If he loved me, he would have taken me with him.

I was left with my mom. I hated this cold-hearted woman who had no clue who we kids were, especially me, who obviously did not love us or want us. I was hated, by her, my own mother, because I so obviously reminded her of him, in every way. I was absolutely terrified of what was to come because I knew we all had a long, fucking hard road ahead. The dragon's head had told me to "buckle up, buttercup"; so I knew I was about to get a lot of shit dumped on me. I was six years old, what the fuck did I know? All I knew was that my life was about to drastically change, and I was smart and intuitive enough to know it was most definitely not for the better.

My life from then on, suffice it to say, was abuse, both emotional and physical—with a lot of neglect as the foundation to a plateau of tragedy and trauma galore. My life growing up was a kaleidoscope of nonconformity: being starved as punishment; locked in my room for lying, stealing, disobeying, getting Bs and Cs in school; and for not agreeing to being adopted by an abusive stepfather, who shoved my face into a hot potpie at the age of eight.

When my mom married this abuser, I refused the adoption. But, if I did not cave, he would adopt no one. My four siblings abused me physically and mentally until I agreed. My mom bribed me, promising me she would allow me to pick a middle name if I told the judge in court that I agreed to the adoption . . . eight-year-old girl . . . middle name of my choice? Uh yeah, I picked the middle name and ended up the starved little girl, locked in a closet. Who knew, you asked? Me. That is who, I respond. The writing was very obviously on the wall and why I resisted for several months. Oddly enough, I was the only one abused by the stepfather.

Looking back, it was not odd at all. I was my birth father's favorite. I had his looks, his mannerisms. I was quintessentially Teddy's daughter. As a child, I could neither see nor understand why. As a woman who has loved and lost, I genuinely understand my mother's loss and anger. My birth father was the love of her life and she felt rage at his abandonment. She felt fear from his leaving, and she felt that she had settled with my stepfather.

My father was a chemist; my stepfather a mechanic. My mother came from a humble background, and she was very much a materialistic person. My birth father came from a strong, wealthy family. My mom never understood she still had that wealth, even without my dad. Everything growing up was about appearances. Our home was the nicest, everyone adored my mother, she was the best nurse, and everyone bragged to me about having her deliver their baby. I always gave a blank look when I heard this because I could not fathom my mom being kind. It was a foreign concept. Again, appearances and faces she put out to the public were deceptive and shallow. My mom spent her energy on people who did not matter and came home empty to the family to whom she should have showered attention, love, and energy. Nothing was ever good enough for my mother. Sadly, she remained a very bitter woman, dying bitter and empty.

***

I repeatedly say I raised myself, sadly. I did not receive attention growing up. I did not have guidance on how to be a young lady or what changes were happening to me. I did get lessons on how to behave. I got lessons on how to appear in public. I got lessons on not to ever, and I mean *ever*, air dirty laundry in public.

I was never taught to cook by her side, or sew, and she was amazing at both things. I learned those skills in school. It was expected of me to do those things in the home. My mom worked, and I had chores; in fact, my sisters and I did all the household work a mom should do. She went to work on the night shift, came home, slept until it was dinnertime, ate, then went back to bed until an hour before she had to leave for her shift. That was my life with my mom growing up. She was a provider, a nag, and I heard from her when I did something wrong. No encouragement, no positive reinforcement, and no life lessons for me to take along my journey.

Did I resent this? Yes. Did I yearn for a mom? Yes. Do I resent her now? No, I do not because I have, along my journey in life, realized that she gave what she was capable of, and it was extremely little. As toxic as she was, I am grateful for the little contact we had.

This woman was so afraid to be alone in her life, she preferred to live with an alcoholic who beat and starved her youngest daughter for twelve years of her life. My mom never laid a hand on me, but she instigated a lot of my abuse.

She never stopped it and looking back, she certainly antagonized it with her antics and anger and rage. The "wait till your father gets home" and complaining to enrage him to take his belt off when he stepped through the door. The calling him at work to tell him I brought a B home on a report card and that she knew I could have done better, and I had given a sarcastic comment in return. The time I had decided enough was enough; I had told her I was going to call the police if either of them had the audacity to put a hand on me again, which got me dragged out of my room by my hair and pulled down thirty stairs into the basement. I was then told to clean it before I could eat dinner. I thought knowing the word "audacity" should give me some credit, but apparently not.

So many nights it was a battle of wills as I sat at the dinner table refusing to drink the milk I was being forced to drink with my meal when she knew I hated milk and had trouble swallowing it without choking and throwing up. Many nights I would be sitting at that same table come 10:00 p.m., when it was time for her to leave for work. That warm, farm-fresh milk still sat there. I was ever-resistant and ready for the beating I knew was coming when my stepfather woke from his nap in the Barcalounger. Many times one of my siblings would take pity on me and sneak in and drink it for me. Kool-Aid, Coke, and other sugary drinks were forbidden in my home. It was milk or water, and for some perverse reason, I was not offered water at dinner. I needed milk to grow strong.

I ran away repeatedly, trying to escape. I was the black sheep in my family—worthless and lawless. Anything that went wrong was blamed on me. Yet, even to this day, I am asked for help and then told to go away. Always asking me for help—yet do not ask me to join anything, do not give me anything, do not praise me for anything, and do not dare to thank me for anything because I am a horrible person. They made things up about me to villainize me. Years of this took a toll until I became left-hand path and did my path work. Now I see it is them, not I, who needs help.

***

This reminds me of a story when I was about ten years old and was sent to my room on Friday afternoon after school. A roll of quarters was stolen from my parents' dresser. Because I had taken change from my mother's coat pocket for school lunch and had admitted it earlier in the week, they felt that it was me who had done it. I was beaten, sent to my room without dinner, and told I would stay there all weekend until I confessed. I was locked in the closet of my room. I refused to budge on this one. I had not stolen the quarter roll. I had admittedly taken the loose change for lunch money she had forgotten to leave out. In my child's mind, that was not theft.

On Sunday, I had still not been fed. I was spent of tears, and beyond hungry. My eldest sister let me out for a bathroom break. The stepfather was at the airport working and my mother was sleeping since she worked the third shift at the hospital. I made a break for it and ran away, stealing an orange as I left the family home, not looking back.

I made it to the grove of willow trees at my elementary school and sat with a coat draped around me, defiant. I read a Trixie Belden mystery book that I had read numerous times, eyeing the orange, thinking how great it was going to taste.

Growing up in an upper-middle-class family is not all it is cracked up to be. Life is beautiful on the outside looking in. We had the beautiful home, the vacations, the etiquette. But the house of horrors and the threats reverberated inside my head repeatedly and stopped me that day from even eating a stolen orange. The "wait until your father gets home" scared me, even as a runaway; "What-if?" and "Will they catch me?" I tried to focus on Trixie to calm the pounding in my heart and head because I was not going home. Ever. I knew me running was going to get me a fracture somewhere on this broken soul and I was just too broken to cope that day.

I sensed him before I saw the man, being hypervigilant. He appeared from nowhere: handsome and distinguished, eyes of cobalt blue, jet black hair. He asked me my name, and why I looked so sad. I was starved for attention back then, and it was the 1970s. I had no shame. I told this man everything. He asked me if I really, truly needed that orange, with his hand out expectantly. I was perturbed. Uh yeah, yeah, I did. I looked calmly at him and asked why. He told me to look inside myself and see a broken boy a little younger than myself walking with a suitcase of sackcloth. I did not bother to tell him I had no idea what sackcloth was at the time. He knew damn well that I did not comprehend that part. I knew he was getting his point across with the fact that the younger kid was carrying a suitcase, which meant he was more serious than me.

I felt hit with lightning bolts of recognition with this kid. Past lives looking back. His mouth had blood pouring down from him biting the inside of his cheek. I knew instinctively that we were in different time periods; the kid was ten years old yet ten years ahead of me. I did not understand that concept then. I understand it now. I looked longingly at that orange and then at the man. Putting Trixie down, I got up and walked to the man. I said, "Here, sir, he needs it more than me, I know."

I kicked my sneaker into the ground and tears welled up but never fell. This man wiped them without ever touching me. He said, "You are not alone, know this. You may fall, you may fear, you may choke, young lady, but you are grace. Nothing in your life is that bitter you cannot tolerate it for a brief period. Go home. Face the music and I promise you this. Not a hand will be put on you today and one day, the Grace you give others will be given to you tenfold. This little boy has no one, and he has not found his Grace. Spaghetti is his name and Spaghetti is his Grace."

I simply nodded and went home. I was not beaten. The police were there. I was lectured by an ignorant cop for scaring my mom. I was sent to my room. The idiot didn't even realize I was not fed. Had he even thought about it, I was on seventy-two hours of no food. Way to go, policeman.

If you know J, you will laugh at the spaghetti reference. He refuses to accept organized religion from his childhood trauma in the name of God. He has the Flying Spaghetti Monster from Pastaferianism as his joke. So, yes, that was Satan who came to me that day and that was J with his suitcase, running away from home. I do not think he ever got far. That is his story to tell, not mine.

***

When I was twenty-four, I woke up from a vision to realize the father I was told was dead was not. I found him, went to meet him, and fell back in love with this amazing man who left his kids he loved behind because I made the decision to eat a bottle of Tylenol as if it was candy. It is more complicated than that, but you get the gist. He was a Satanist back then and he had his own journey to take. I had asked my siblings if they wanted to reach out and talk to Dad. My eldest brother sadly was too angry, and my dad died a year later.

Ironically, in 2017, my eldest brother reached out to me to ask hundreds of questions about him. Oddly, I am hated by my family, but they come to me to fix their mistakes. Yet, I am excluded from their lives. I am a pariah. What they do not understand is that I do not care. I will help because I feel sorry for them and their ignorance.

My brother did not want contact with my dad because he believed my mom's lies. After her death, he opened our adoption papers and her divorce papers. Lo and behold, the truth came out. He then wanted to know about Dad. I gave my brother his answers because I am that person. I hold no grudges.

My father would have wanted him to be given the things he asked about and for. It is not about holding things over people's heads and being harsh; I do not treat my family as they treat me. I tend to take the high road and give what they ask, not expecting anything in return, and then I move on. I find that it is the right thing to do, and it is their loss not having me in their lives. I am a good person and the fact they do not see that is on them, not on me. I genuinely feel lighter not having them in my life because I truly feel they did not make my life easy growing up, and they never once tried to make amends for what they did to me, or tried to even acknowledge what was done to me. I am good with the pariah status.

When I found my dad, he was living sober as a campground host in a town in Washington State. Alone. He had never remarried. He had left us in Maine, resigned to divorce my mom and abandon his children. He was told we wanted nothing to do with him when he had begged to come home a few weeks later. He signed divorce papers and turned over his parental rights, a broken man. Few people realize this about my dad, Teddy, but he never knew who his father was. He had a son from a marriage during the Korean War, who he had to leave behind and a daughter from a marriage that ended in divorce. She was murdered a year before I was born by an off-duty police officer in Florida. His luck with children was not the best. It is sad because he gave the best love, attention, and education any man could as a father. He was patient and kind and loving, and he should not have lost his children.

The woman who raised me with the man she allowed to assist was an abusive alcoholic who beat me and broke me over stupid things like coming home fifteen minutes late, getting a B on a report card, forgetting a report card on a Friday in my school locker, or not vacuuming the floor properly at nine years old. Telling a silly, childish lie got me locked in a closet for a weekend without food. There was no children's protective services to rescue me. I ran away repeatedly, only to get dragged home and lectured by policemen about scaring my mom. I begged our neighbors to let me live with them. Everyone knew what I was enduring, but back in the 1970s people did not interfere.

The judge who decided she was the best fit should be disbarred. However, hindsight is 20/20, isn't it? My mom played the victim perfectly until her death. I did not attend that deathbed scene nor her funeral. I said my goodbyes years before, tired of being cast as the villain in her draconian plays.

During my dad's absence he had travelled to Texas, met the Maharishi, and found his center again. He went to Venice Beach, California, and spent time meditating in a Buddhist sanctuary before ending up in Washington State, where he practiced his spiritual path of Satanism and pushed on. My uncles kept him abreast of us children but never let on to us that he was still alive. I went out to meet him again and stayed with him during his final year.

He was diagnosed with prostate cancer the year I found him, which spread quickly through his spine and into his brain. He died eighteen months later. Those eighteen months were amazing. We bonded and renewed our relationship as father and daughter while hiking, camping, and fishing up and down the mountains, valleys, and rivers of Washington State. His death did not break me. It built me up because I knew our time was special and a gift. The Spirit world gave me that time with my dad as a lesson to learn. I just did not know how to apply it then, but now I do.

Despite what I have been through I do not hold grudges. Grudges are for the weak. Grudges only cause cancers of the mind and spirit and hold us back from Godhood. Anger and resentment cause us harm. The person we resent sleeps well at night while we fester. I let things go. What if I have anger and they deserve in my heart a punishment? Destruction spells and rituals work wonders. However, I have the patience of a saint and do not mind waiting decades for revenge. I do not care if you are of the same bloodline. What you reap, you shall sow, and what you cause? You shall reward yourself in my time, not your own.

I have walked away from a mother, siblings, spouse, and children who have done me wrong. Not because I was weak and could not handle it but because I knew that I did everything I could to fix the situation and they were not up to par. They were unwilling to fix the situation, right the wrongs, or work on themselves or on us. That was enough for me not to waste my breath, time, effort, or energy on things I could not change, people who did not love, and things that did not want to be fixed. I would rather expend energy and love on things I can fix, change, and heal. Evil can be good, and Evil can be bad. You must figure out your definition, your limit, and what you can thrive on.

Chapter 3
Defining Moment

The second defining moment in the left-hand path for me was when I was pushed to overdose. I am a strong person. I always, as a Celtic Holly, Leo with Capricorn Rising and Aquarius Moon and Pisces in my North Node, pushed myself to excel.

However, I was pushed to the edge of sanity by a man . . . not a lover, a traitor—stalked and harassed, a story not to be told just yet. I overdosed with my phone off in a hotel room by taking fifty 10mg Flexeril. I hallucinated for three days. Demonic eyes in the room kept me alive, talking to me and pushing me to breathe when I was not able to on my own.

Every friend I had in the world had shut me out because of lies told by this stalker. I was exhausted and refused to explain. I asked myself, "Why bother?" Most of my friends tried to support me, but I shut them out, knowing if they stuck by me, they too would become victims like the few who were staunch supporters and were already getting hit publicly.

Now I realize Azazel, the Physician, and Satan sat with me for three days while the drugs ran their course. On the third day, I was found and brought to a psychiatric hospital. The level was still toxic. I survived to fight another day, and then my recovery and self-discovery journey began. I was villainized by everyone, or so I thought; I chose to not fight publicly while I had to survive privately simply because someone wanted to become famous. That is all I will say, they deserve no press from me and lies cannot be explained or justified.

***

In October 2022, I realized I was wanting. I did a meditation and asked a Luciferian to do an initiation ritual for me after reading *Apotheosis: The Ultimate Beginner's Guide to Luciferianism & the Left-Hand Path* by Michael W. Ford, but I felt screwed over at the time because the altar was clean. It made me feel that Luciferianism was not for me, and I needed to branch into Satanism, which was the path that was right for me. I felt she did not do the ritual. Warning! If the photo you receive as "evidence of ritual" is TOO CLEAN . . . IT IS A FUCKING FAKE!!!! My altar is dirty, messy, and used. All my altars. You never mix altars either, by the way. She did that to me too, not realizing I was involved in witchcraft for years. Adept and a master at what I do, I chose to come to her and not do the work myself. TSK TSK. Satanists do not turn the other cheek, and we certainly like to mix up destruction on a platter, do we not?

During my meditation, Satan came to me, and the following was shared on Samhain night:

Your journey must start now. Do the ritual and stand your ground with J. If you two cannot get things together as a couple, you cannot be a couple for now. You matter too, LuciaBelia, even though recently, you have forgotten this. You have been so busy chasing your tail like the asp eating itself, consumed with chasing him.

You must now focus on your business and create your website. Call it: "Satan's Eye of the Storm," for you are my eye of the storm. Start your studies. Become adept, become the master. Do you want our help? Do the work. Get up and running. Stop being lazy and helpless. You are not fear-based, and you have forgotten yourself. This is not who you are. You have both lost your way and until you remember who you are, you cannot be one. Three cannot be one, can they, LuciaBelia? We gave you two lives together in perfect harmony in the beginning because you were anchors. A symphony of power, life, love, and support. Your storm blew in and you both got lost in M's storm of power. Get your strength back and find your way back or forever be lost in her lies and chaos. The choice is yours. Rise, rise, rise to the occasion, or forever be lost.

What happened to you? What happened between you? If you find yourself, you find your path, you will find him. What is the most important thing to you right now, LuciaBelia? Your life has become empty because you are not healing people, and your destiny is not being fulfilled. You stopped working and that is your destiny. He will come back if you move forward. We promise this to you.

Give us your time, your energy, your work, your skills, and your passions. Show us you are a worthy adversary. Learn your Demonic Magick. Learning is key. Find your mentor in the storm of this chaos. You are the eye. The storm is the key. If you sit in silence for just a moment, you will figure it out and solve our puzzle. The puzzle will unfold. You have weeks to figure it out and master yourself to bring him back and to become adept, not years like most, but you of all people can do it. People will doubt you, laugh at you, and even tell you that you are insane. They will put barriers up. They will judge you and test you. Push through it, LuciaBelia, and care not because they are not at your level. They wish they were skilled as you. Only one is more powerful than you and only he can test you, but you will pass his tests. Do not judge him. He has been failed many times. Laugh if you must, but do not judge. He will help you, but he will not coddle you in the long run. You are tough and you can handle his bullshit. Show your strength and back him in a corner when you must.

You are a master of all things. Trust yourself. Trust your instincts. Do not care if people think you are crazy about this. Twelve weeks you have. J will be back. People will question your methods. They will question why you want him back. We took him away so you can learn to appreciate what we gave you in the first place. Value a soulmate, value it over the fear of abandonment. Value your worth over issues of loss and self-depreciation. You learn this and you can have what you want. Until then? Suffer the consequences of your reckless behavior. You do not value much in your life materialistically. You ask for little. Your biggest asset you value is J, so it is what we hold as the biggest prize for you. He is miserable without you, and he values you most. You both need to learn not to allow others to push you to extremes and to put each other above fears. Did I not give you the love of your life as you asked when you were working hard? Yes, you were doing something noble, and you stopped. Now, start it again.

You feed off each other's hunger and strength. A yin to the yang. The other inside out. Teaching each other and growing together. He taught you love; you taught him patience in forgiveness. It will be back, but not until you learn to do what we have asked. Finish the Gatekeeper's challenge and figure out you can make it happen by force, if necessary. There is a riddle about the Gatekeeper. If you can solve it, you can be reunited. Until then, you are stuck. Can you figure out the trap most fail on?

Letting go to get a hold. You are the few among the many at my table feasting. Do the work daily. The calm before the storm ends up as the eye of the storm: grounded, centered, fearless, and fallen into the abyss of bright darkness. Figure out the riddled conundrum and he will be yours by ritual and by force if you want.

This meditation was the catapult to my active search for a mentor. I was having issues in my relationship. I was stagnant in my business. I was not happy in general with Druidic life— eclectic more than Druidic because I stepped into Santeria, the

Old Ones, Black Magick, White Magic, whatever I felt led to do. I did magic mixed with life coaching. I truly was adrift at this point, trying to figure out where I was going and what I wanted to do; trying to decide if my partner and I were going to Ukraine; putting me and my life on hold for our joint mission was a major distraction. We were down to the wire on decisions that were affecting my life but about which he was willy-nilly. The resentment was real to say the least.

The road for us had always been easygoing and respectful, but after the one who shall remain nameless had done her evil, we were fighting, bickering, and not as supportive as we normally would be, and I saw what Satan was saying during my channeled meditation.

Here is the thing. If you are adept, and Magick is your life? You are Magick. It is what you breathe. It is what you live for. You question nothing regarding it. WHAT THE FUCK, you say? Part of being left-hand path (LHP) is that we question everything, right? Right. I do not question what I know to be true. Within me, of me and Magick, I personally do not question demons when I know through my gift it is true. Why waste my breath, time, and energy just because the LHP says I should? I would rather expend my energy on changing my circumstance, or healing the outcome, than beating my chest and crying "why?"

I knew in that channeled meditation with Satan that:

> 1. All will be if I serve him. Kneel before him, serve him, so it is done. I am the power of abundance and understand my own light. The magistrate says to kneel, so I kneel. Greatness comes when I let go of things I

can't control, realize I am what and who I am, and let people go who do not serve me.

2. I needed to stop justifying myself. Stop accepting excuses and mistreatment when I know that I deserve better. Not because J was doing it intentionally; he never hurt me intentionally, he did the best he could. He was not in a place to do better. I was making unreasonable demands on a person already working 120-hour weeks and serving two Gods . . . so to speak, he could not reasonably please me too. No matter how much in love with me he was, I was being unfair.

I had to find the mentor mentioned in my channeling. I had twelve weeks to rise to the challenge. I always meet a challenge and land on my feet, and this was going to be no different for me. Not just for J and me, but for my own sanity. I created the website, "Satan's Eye Of The Storm" that day and filed the necessary LLC documents with the state. I was not fucking around. I surfed the web looking for a mentor and sent out a few emails, surfed a few groups and chatted with a few people. No one stood out. Until I found *Become A living God*. I knew E.A. Koetting was who I was being referred to. People laughed at me and said, "Good luck, sweetie. Do you think you are going to get E.A. Koetting to take the time to mentor you? Boy, do you really think you are important." Yes, I do think I am important. Isn't that the entire point of being? To value your worth? To cherish yourself and to choose you?

I emailed E.A. and booked a consultation. Let me tell you this about E.A. Koetting: he is one of the humblest men I have ever met. He did laugh at me when I told him what I wanted to do. He told me it takes ten years to reach mastery level in Demonic Magick at the beginning of our conversation. Ok, he did not laugh at me; he chuckled and said it would be extremely difficult. We agreed to do a ritual the following Tuesday for abundance and prosperity to see where it led and meet up again the following Thursday. By the end of the call, he was excited for me. He felt I could do it and was encouraging.

When I received the video of my ritual of King Paimon from E.A. Koetting I rolled with laughter. Why? Because during our first consultation I told him repeatedly that Satan liked to interrupt all invocations and meditations I had with other entities, especially Asmodeus. He had even said during the consultation that he found Satan talking over spirit. During the Ritual, Satan did exactly that. In the end, he ruled that ritual over King Paimon, and he decided what was going to happen next, in my opinion. I'm not taking away from the powers of King Paimon in any way because I greatly benefitted from that ritual, in the spiritual and prosperity sense as well, but Satan and his input, in the end, determined my next steps.

Moving forward, I started weekly mentoring sessions with E.A., and they have become invaluable to me. The guidance, knowledge, and wisdom he has imparted is the biggest reason I am where I am within the sixteen-week budget I was allotted. He has kept me sane during times of upheaval and revelations that would cause most to question their sanity. He has patiently and kindly guided my path, from toddler to queen and graciously given me tools, advice, and time above and beyond mentoring. I will never forget that.

I bought many of his published works but decided not to read them until I had done the work of each Gatekeeper because I did not want to be slanted or prejudiced to the Gatekeeper or his opinion of the Gatekeeper prior to doing my own work. To thy own self be true, right? I had E.A. do a Deification Ritual when I was ready, and I felt immensely empowered by this ritual. During this ritual, Andrieh Vitemus sent me a sigil to call Nyx, the Goddess of Darkness, and I felt immediately called to this. E.A. also explained things during this time of heightened gifts that were already extremely powerful and how I would continue to see growth of ability. I was feeling, at times, like I was hit by a freight train. I was working eighteen hours a day. Preparation for my path was not an easy task.

Chapter 4
The Beginning of the Gatekeepers' Quest

While this was going on, I was being passed from one Gatekeeper to the next. Each Gatekeeper had a purpose for me, a puzzle I had to solve to get to the next. Demonic Gatekeepers do not play around with you. They are there with you to heal, to teach, to train, and to destroy. That could mean destroying bad habits, removing things which no longer serve you or people who should not be in your life, or bringing people to you that need to be in your life.

The list of benefits of the Gatekeepers is endless if you work them as they should be worked. If you call the Gatekeepers and hold them at arm's length, afraid of them, resisting? You are not ready; walk away, that is my best advice. You are wasting your time and theirs. They truly do not like to have their time wasted. They add value to your life, so why resist? I launched into this wholeheartedly because I recognized that I was about to enter a phase of my life that I had been waiting for since I was four years old, and I could not wait. Eager anticipation does not begin to describe it. I would say a kid at Christmas, but I never had that experience. I am going to say a lover waiting on her first kiss.

I learned about the depth of Candle Magick truly gazing and calling Azazel. I found Azazel as a Dragon's Head, with dazzling yellow eyes hanging suspended above me. I realized I knew this man from childhood. I was not afraid. I have had a deadly fear of snakes since childhood. I realized it was tied to the overdose and his presence during my father's departure and have since been able to let it go with the path work Azazel and I have done together. Prior to that? I could not see a snake on TV or in a pet store without freezing and not breathing—it was that deep of a fear. Sayeth Azazel,

---

You are not the first I sent to the desert, and you will not be the last. Your journey is fraught with crossroads, you find unfair, LuciaBelia. That is your path through hell to ascension. Some fight drugs and alcohol. You have tough decisions to make in the next coming weeks and months that determine the rest of your life, and your choices may seem cold to some. Maybe even selfish, yet for the few come many after, and the sacrifice comes your reward. What you think you are letting go of and walking away from is only a small piece of the grand puzzle. You will see from a different angle at a different crossroad in a few days or weeks. Stay your path, let no questions crush your head. What is done is done with energy. What is the right, oops, left pathway. Go in peace, so shall it be, so shall it be.

At this point in time, I started to meditate on the dragon's head. There was a lot of trickery going on, and I was told by Azazel to cast the snakes out of my home. Lies and deceit: betrayed by people I trusted to remove

everyone from my old life and to only allow them back in when they passed the test of honesty.

I knew with J and I not speaking, I had to make a stand. It was time to let go and move on. I could not do that without betraying him, because I was not able to move on without answers. His silence—his inability to heal or to give closure—was killing me. He was not doing it on purpose; he would never hurt me intentionally. I was the love of his life. I realized that I had to confront J, or whither within. I got this while working with Azazel. I knew if I did not do this, I would dishonor myself. I would also break a promise to J, an unspoken commitment. It was either harm him or harm me. I had a choice to make. Go to him after weeks of silence, confront and destroy our future—or forever hurt. Do or die.

I chose me. Yet again, I was that seven-year-old girl, locked in the closet, starved, and shut out from the family. Deprived of all communication and wrapped in a blanket of silence as punishment for an unknown, unspoken crime. I was, in fact, dying a slow death of unknown origins. I was rapidly dropping weight I could ill afford, not focusing on me. I followed Azazel and his advice. I confronted his silence knowing I was betraying him; knowing I was destroying our future and betraying the love of my life. There were so many lies being told to both of us and we were lost at sea. I needed answers for me. I went to his door. A betrayal to him. I was calm. I left with the answer I needed, and I instantly made life-altering change. My anchor finally started to lay back down, and I stopped drifting aimlessly. The sadness in his eyes when he gave me my answers hurt us both.

I lived a few miles from his home and did not want to pass it daily. I changed cars the day after I confronted him on his porch. I signed a new lease the day after that and was completely moved out three days later. I do not play when it's time to implement a demonic game plan. I had to show J his silence was not tolerated. His silence was from his inability to process, but it was still not acceptable, and the line was drawn. So mote it be, so shall it be until we meet again, my love, my soul, my best friend.

***

It was time for the Gatekeepers' ritual to be performed by E.A. The time and date got confused because I had a boot camp going on. I had a client in town, and E.A. was booked by me to do a ritual for this client. The morning the ritual was scheduled to be done, I was summoned into my scrying mirror by the Gatekeepers. This was not a bad thing; I had been asked the previous Friday by E.A. to pick three Gatekeepers as possible patrons. I had struggled. I had picked Azazel and Satan but could not decide between Ba'al and Belial. Asmodeus was in the back of my head, but something was telling me, "Uhhh, no." At 2:30 a.m., I answered the summons with a bit of trepidation. What did I do wrong? Even adepts worry at times.

Chapter 5
Scrying, Meetings, and Trying

I was scrying in my mirror; all nine Gatekeepers were there. I asked why and what was happening because I knew in my heart E.A. was rescheduling my Gatekeepers' ritual. I was asking if I had mistakenly chosen the patrons. I had a funny relationship with these nine Demons. The nine Demonic Powers were sitting on their thrones in darkness, but a fire was lit between us. They were sitting semi-circular, and each one had an almost ethereal glow behind them. I could more sense than see pieces and glimpses of each one, as if they were tempting and teasing, like a test almost. When I asked what was going on Satan said,

You summoned this meeting, LuciaBelia; it's time for the next leg of your journey. Azazel and I have done what we needed to do, and you know what is next. You must push through urgently; you must push on, for many are depending on you. J is depending on you desperately, for it's time. You must pick, you must pick now. We've been with you every step; we've given you the best of the best. You are my Eastern star rising. You are my eye of the storm. Rise up, LuciaBelia, rise and declare yourself. Pick now; all will be revealed as soon as you do so.

I closed my eyes, and I pushed my third eye into the mirror. I looked deeply into the smoky obsidian mirror I used to scry. I saw all nine men on their thrones, staring expectantly at me: Asmodeus with his smirk; Azazel as a Dragon's Head, patient and kind; Lucifer with his incandescent light; Lucifuge and that logbook; Belial and his knowing glance; Satan and his loving kindness; Abaddon and his expecting way; Beelzebub and his wisdom; Ba'al and his knowledge ready to be dispersed, all expecting my answer. All patient, in cavernous areas with paths leading into their dark underworld, many distant lights behind them, a hub of activity in the distance behind each showing their realm. I heard their worlds softly in the background, teasing and tantalizing me to form a decision.

I say clearly, "I choose Belial."

He beams with pride and says,

I am here, I am here, I am here . . . Let us begin, LuciaBelia. Your foundational belief in yourself is fully broken. It's destroyed, removed, gone. You dropped into the abyss, love versus mind versus knowledge and worth versus deserve versus receive—very in love, but you're settled. You've committed a cardinal sin. You had magic done when you were broken and not thinking. He too was broken and both undeserving. Both needed to be healed. Both lost and now realize loss. You are ready to have quality. The break is healing like a bone; he will come if you can have love. We had to employ tough love to you before to say you will never have love again. You were a toddler once, to us you are a toddler again, learning to walk the Demonic Path. You are one of us, you will always be our child, LuciaBelia. We saved you years ago, you became our Guardian. We will always treat you as one of our own. When a child has been naughty, they get punished to learn valuable lessons. Gone, but not forever—a time-out, so to speak.

We had to tell you that to make you dig in and do the work. Drink in me, LuciaBelia. The darkness, breathe it in. Absorb in every sense the wet, the dry, the density, for it is you. It will, and it is, becoming you; you are the conundrum, bringing your race into the maze, a path of thick darkness of light. You will guide people to the pods. Azazel and I are Satan as well, not unknown. Everybody thinks it, but they're not sure. We are unnamed. We reveal to you in ways you can comprehend, not in our real selves.

Ask yourself, "why is Asmodeus a cross-legged gentleman drinking fine whiskey YOU like when he is kind and loving yet dark and sinister when he is wrath and destruction?" Everyone sees things to their understanding, right? You, dear LuciaBelia, are different because you see beyond normal sight, you see beyond explanation and judgment, everything for you is GEOMETRIC. Trapezoid, right?

*You self-correct. You are on a trajectory; we need you for
this mission to work. The time is almost near. I need you
to make a few more changes.*

*As you grow and blossom, this will create an unfreezing
of your heart. You give freely, but you do not receive well.
You must learn to receive freely. Insist on receiving. You
insist on others receiving from you—turn that around
on yourself now. You are gracious and kind, but not to
yourself. Stop punishing yourself for what others put on
you.*

That sounds easy right? No, that has been the hardest
change to date with the Gatekeepers, actually. Accepting gifts
from others. Accepting love. I have only ever accepted from J.
That was monumental—me opening to others—and that was
because of Belial.

---

*You are not a manifester. You simply are. You simply get,
surround, and receive moving forward. It is a part of
you. There is a great envy of your evil empire to come.*

That was Belial's puzzle for me. I had to stop and think about
that one. It is true. I never worry about money. I occasionally will
do an abundance or prosperity ritual, but it is generalized—not
simply for wealth but health, love, and all things. I always have
what I need, when I need it, at my fingertips. When I went to get
a new car? I did not worry about a car loan; it materialized, and
it was for the car I wanted and needed. I do not live check-to-

check; I live comfortably in a lovely home on the mountainside with a ninety-mile view. I have lovely neighbors with an amazing caretaker who is like a second father to me and a landlord who comes up from Boston once a month and lives in his apartment downstairs. I cook for both whenever they let me. It is a great life I have here, and it is because I have opened my heart as Belial has asked me to receive love from others.

> *The Phenix rises healing light candescent, whisper during my Gatekeeper ritual.*

> *Satan, Belial, Lucifuge, Azazel, Asmodeus, all offered to be my patron. I chose Asmodeus. I feared him the most because he was most like me. I feared my wrath, anger, and destructive ways. I also chose Lucifuge as a patron because I asked if I could have two. I was told that, in this special circumstance, I was allowed. In my demonic birth chart, both were equal and since five stepped forward, I was told I was special and so I could work with two patrons.*

***

During my Gatekeepers' Ritual, my mentor—whom as I mentioned previously, I adore beyond belief and is the reason why I believe I have come so far, so fast—E.A. told me I had to let go of three fears: the fear of abandonment, the fear of going crazy, and the fear of people not liking me. I should step on anyone in my way. I laughed at this because it was exactly what I had been told the night before. If you ever doubt E.A. and his ability, you should really stop. He and I are very in sync with

our visions and what he brings to me in our mentoring is pretty much what has just come out in my meditation the prior night or morning.

I have realized a balance of perfection and peace on the path with the Gatekeepers: of peace, love, and harmony, as well as wrath and destruction. I realize that's why I had to pick both Asmodeus and Lucifuge. It took me several days to fully understand that. Oddly enough, the shadow within me was not fear; it was the excitement of what I was capable of. It was anticipation combined with awe and understanding that Asmodeus represented the balance of everything I am capable of when I do not hold back. I am so used to being reserved and Asmodeus's biggest lesson for me during my journey was not to hold back. Let it out. Let go and let loose. Stop being afraid of what people believe. My reality as a God is all that matters.

E.A. suggested I get a demonic chart reading with Right Reverend Bill Duvendack, and as mentioned, Asdmodeus and Lucifuge were equal. I started a journey with the lovely Right Reverend Bill Duvendack as well. During my card reading, eight out of ten cards were fire, death, and rebirth. The cards showed challenges and victory. The last card was the Tower card. Let me tell you, I have no fear. I am used to abrupt changes. I thrive in chaos. I trust my instinct and I trust myself. I do not question things I am told unless I know it to be a lie, a misdirect, or incorrect. When it rings true in my heart, my soul, or my being, I go with it. Being a discerner, I go with it. I know when I am being lied to or misled, it is a gift. Some people say trust and verify. I say do and do not bother unless I must, and may Satan

help you if I must bother to verify. It is going to get a whole lot of ugly up in here . . .

You may ask, "Why have a mentor then?" Because I am told to by the same Gatekeepers I trust, love, and respect. My journey is not complete without his tutelage. He has brought immense wisdom and guidance to me. I would not be able to complete this herculean task of mastering the Gatekeepers in twelve weeks and be sane without him, his support, his guidance, his advice, and mentoring.

Before getting passed to the next Gatekeeper, I was feeling a bit lost at this point because J was an extension of me. I could not lose momentum. I was taking INLP Hypnosis courses. I was giving Bootcamp for Life coaching. I was moving. I was shaking. I was not giving up an inch of ground. It was okay to be sad for my loss, but I was not going backwards. Feeling lost at this moment and feeling betrayed by all I held dear in my personal life, I had a personal consultation with BlackWitchCoven.com. She confirmed that J and I were twin soulmates, that we were supposed to be together, and there was a lot of magical bs being done to us. She suggested a few cut and clears, to let the dust settle and let him resolve his confused thoughts. I had also taken her demonology course to progress my knowledge of the Ars Goetia faster. She is amazing. Take the course if you have not.

I decided to reach out and contact several women in the LHP who were moving and shaking. A few were not for me; we were not moving in the same direction. I met with Jennifer of Belladonna Botanicals. She was delightful and had a lot of factual knowledge and growth. I enjoyed meeting LilithCult on Etsy, a

real gem of a Luciferian from Spain: extremely knowledgeable
and trustworthy. If you are asking, why do you, as a master
healer, go to someone else? Sometimes, an attorney has a fool
for a client. Sometimes, a physician has a fool for a patient too.

It is funny how it works, these Demons deciding who to
bring together. Myself, E.A., Blackwitchcoven, Right Reverend
Bill Duvendack, Martin McGreggor, and then I find a lovely
treasure on Etsy with ClaviculaNoxBoutique. 777 and I have
bonded and become great friends and I cannot wait to see him
at the LHP convention. He is the most generous, kind soul I
have ever met. His treasures are pure genius. I have loved our
engagements. Creating my altar with his art and chemistry
and his findings has been a pure joy for me. My journey with
Razvan in the Netherlands at Forgotten Engravings has forged a
friendship I can never lose. This LHP journey has been a great
ride with the building of friendships along the way. I recall now
Satan telling me when I fell into the abyss that no one would be
there to catch me, but many would be there after I fell. I had to
let many people go when I went LHP because they did not serve
me or wished me ill, but the people I have met—the kindness,
the authenticity, and the amazing grace I have been given with
these friendships—is worth all the gold in the world.

We, as practitioners, should not attempt our own healings.
I personally do not do my own healing rituals. If you choose to
do yours, that is awesome. I believe in self-care. This is my self-
care and self-love to have others do rituals for me. I often do
not do my own love rituals, healing rituals, or protection rituals
when they are extremely important, for multiple reasons: one,

if I am low on energy, why risk it; two, I like to engage with others and sometimes you just need to go to someone with a higher mastery to get the job done or with less involvement than yourself. As a master/adept, you should know when to ask for help, and if you are not smart enough to ask for help, this is not the line of work for you.

This life is not an easy life. I do not "practice Demonic Magick." It is an extension of my soul, of my very being, of my essence. When I made the decision to drink and breathe in the darkness, it became a part of me. When there is a disease within me, I have no issue asking for help, or getting a second opinion. That does not mean I am going to run house to house to house getting opinions and healings. That is a waste of energy and resources.

Our community in the LHP is fractured. Everyone has set their Kingdom up, their empire. I have a path; I have a plan that Satan and the Gatekeepers have blazing for me. I know a part of that is unification of the truth. We must unite to survive what is coming. Those with true gifts really must learn to trust and depend upon each other, to work together for common good, because as E.A. says, "The storm is coming." Where we end up when that storm hits is up to us.

Ba'al is about connections, about creating, and bonding, about getting out and meeting and bonding and blazing your Kingdom through bonding. No man is an island, no queen or king can have a kingdom without sitting at the table of others and experiencing their joy. You learn from others and learning is growth. We all have a purpose in the LHP and if we live closed off, nothing can be accomplished in our own kingdom.

I realize that I am a demonic healer; I am the conduit to healing, as much as I am the conduit between my peers. I can choose to do this through the eye of Satan's storm of calmness, or I CAN be the conduit of the destructive storm that brings peace afterwards. I always have the choice of which conduit I bring to the table.

Chapter 6
The Weeping Prophets Come to Call

L ucifuge Rofocale was an amazing experience. I was passed
to this Deity: the King of the Underworld, the Keeper of the
Books.

I was known as a child to weep while sitting in church, in
the presence of the Holy Spirit. Raised as a Roman Catholic,
self-raised in the church by a mother who was excommunicated,
I walked myself to mass. I found solace in the church. During
times of hardship throughout life, I would sit in an empty chapel
and light a candle and talk to the spirit and tears would roll
down my face. My family teased me and called me the weeping
prophet.

When I summoned Lucifuge Rofocale, I wept silent tears.
Many tried to tell me when this happened, I was unloading
emotional baggage. It could be partially true because this
demonic powerhouse will break you of anything that no longer
serves you.

However, during a ritual meditation on the same day and
time that the Right Reverend Bill Duvendack was performing a
pact with Lucifuge for me, I was summoned to a Gatekeepers'
meditation for peaceful thought and guidance, and I called
Lucifuge to it. After I had summoned the elements and was
summoning Lucifuge, I heard snickering from the East. It was

Lucifer and Asmodeus. I turned, with tears of elation on my face, and stopped the ritual to say, "I am NOT WEAK with these tears, gentlemen. I am a Fucking GOD!!! These are tears of pure spiritual appreciation and do not for one moment snicker, thinking me weak. I love and respect this demon and he touches my soul with his mere presence," The snickering stopped, and we proceeded.

They knew what was happening, of course, but they were gently reminding me to harness that energy and power rather than expend it. My mentor said the same thing when we discussed it. I laughed because I realized in hindsight Asmodeus and Lucifer, in their way, were saying exactly that: to harness that energy and not release it with tears, to make my energy more potent.

I cry tears when angry, never when sad. I realized that day it is my body's way of imploding the release of endorphins to not physically explode my rage on people, to balance me so that I do not become violent. It was an inability to express the rage adequately. I instantly knew that the Demons had shot knowledge into me with path work on how to deal with rage boiling under the surface, how to harness it to my advantage, to effectively cope with it, to utilize it to my advantage and to not waste it unnecessarily. I tend to not show emotions. I have a great resting bitch face and do not anger easily. I let a lot go because people are not worth getting upset over; I look at the outcome versus the moment more than the instant gratification. I also look at the intentions behind actions before I react. Not a very Leo trait but I am not a big believer that you are solely your sun sign.

What was prevalent during this meditation was Lucifuge asking me, "Am I to not to love myself first and trust them to do as promised?" I am not lonely if I do my work; loneliness is only a passing thought, and I am complete within.

I'm not the little girl in the closet anymore, locked in, hungry and afraid of the dark. I now embrace the darkness. I am a beacon to the dark and an emissary of its light. I am not the little girl who has gone without food. I am not living in the shadow of death, but walk amongst the dead and the living, deciding who to help because I can and will give and I choose to receive.

I am a grown girl who does not need love. I am the woman who desires to give and receive love. I am the eternal flame from within that lights the world; because I am one with the eternal dark flame burning dark, yet bright, within me—a mystery yet known.

I can hold that flame pure—no one is going to give me the love that I need or desire until I decide it is time, because I cannot have three layers of love in my flame.

I can only have one pure flame, and if my flame is fractured, there is no pure love. However, if I turn my perspective and look at things from a different angle, I can see things clearly and what was once three is now perfectly joined together dancing to it, so beautiful, glorious, and perfectly aflame in darkness and light.

There is no room for anything or anybody. Complete from the tip to the base, dancing in harmony, it is everything. It shows perfect and complete on my own and is identical to Leviathan to Asmodeus to Lucifuge to Lucifer into chaos. Each one of my elemental candles is perfectly in sync. How beautiful is it to get this affirmation that each candle's flame is in tune, in alignment, equal and pure, joined and I know I AM. I know him, and he IS.

OK, show me my way, show me my past. What is next? What is next? I have no fear. I have total faith in what I am doing and what I must do next. I put one foot in front of the other and I do the task in front of me. I follow my intuition. Show me the magic, show me the way. It's so beautiful! Everybody thinks the darkness is an abyss, but they don't yet place in their head and heart simultaneously that the darkness is pure peace. It is so bright here. I don't want to leave, dancing amongst the candle flames, jumping from wick to wick. Leaping, like a ballerina from flame to flame to flame eternally— Lucifuge playing violin as I am pirouetting around in the underworld through each chamber, seeing life replay my trauma and drama without a care. I clearly see what was done, what I have done, it is not careless of me. I have absorbed it. I am only separated from the impact of it and can see the changes I have made and the healing I have done. It is not opening old wounds. It shows me where I was and how far I have come and where I need yet to go to be the Empress they need me to be. Gracious, graceful, healing. Destructive and evil. I am a light in pure darkness. I am the conundrum no one knows the answer to quite yet. I know. I know the name. I know the path and I know the way. All things are revealed. Things I should not have known are now revealed and I cannot unknow what was said. Lucifuge, with his ethereal beauty and his wisdom, looks upon me with such great sadness at what is to come. He tells me my travels are great and my burden is heavy, but for such a small one, I will be good and strong and with the three in one I can do this task.

You can look at your past, at the things that caused you scars. If you watch the movie of your life unfold, the trauma and the drama are the things that shape you. I am in the underworld right now and I'm seeing the movie of my life. Me jumping off the fifteen-foot slide. Then overdosing as a four-year-old.

I survived overdosing in my forties for three days, turning through an abyss, dancing around the chambers of the underworld, watching my movie screen because that's what it is when you have no fear: life is a movie screen. It's degrees of separation confronting your past and seeing it like a movie. You can watch what's happened to you and understand why.

It can no longer harm you once you address the shadow. Nobody has power over you to trigger you. That is what

I have learned working with Lucifuge Rofocale, that once you come to the underworld, you watch the movie of your life, and you see things of your past. If you change your perspective and you watch your movie screen and you see things from a different point of view, you see the people who hurt you in your past, your present, and sometimes even in your future. You see your parts of it, and you see their parts and their issues and drama. I was told to do a guided-hypnosis meditation for each Gatekeeper and what they do for people to help them cross their abyss. It is not unique, as I said. Everyone does it. Lucifuge said it is unique to you.

Simply by changing your perspective and looking at things with a different eye, you're able to let it go and rise above, and when you rise above, you're no longer the victim, you're the God. When you're the God, you are the mind, body, and soul of your actions and your consequences. Your actions are your reactions as well. People say your actions have consequences. Your reactions have consequences too.

Be responsible, step up, show no fear, do not care, step on things. My mentor told me during my Gatekeeper ritual, "Do not fear people's reactions to you and know they fear you and your ability and stop caring. Step on them if you must to accomplish your goals, rather than step around them, when necessary." I was told "to stop being afraid of going insane and to stop letting people treat me like I was crazy because of my gifts and to stop caring what people thought of me."

I weighed that very carefully and I don't care what people think about me anymore. It wasn't an overnight process. Letting go is, in and of itself, a process of time. It is a choice you make daily. You open your eyes and decide . . . today, I am going to continue to let it go.

I have no resistance to the Gatekeepers if they asked me to do something. I contemplate it because I am a God, but I understand their motives are for my best interest and for the greater good. Not to mention my growth. I find it ridiculous people come to Demonic Magick for growth then resist the help they are given.

I understand this is about a mission: a plan to do something greater than myself alone could ever do. It has to do with the two worlds joining forces and combining. I do admit, I resisted them taking my twin soulmate away. Even if it is, as they keep telling me, a temporary thing. It hurts my heart to be apart from him. I have come to terms with it with every Gatekeeper. I know, with every one of them, I have asked why. Resistance . . . yet not, because I push forward and do what they ask, despite the sadness and hurt. I have not caved. I have not been broken. I have risen to the challenges they have given me of becoming an adept, a Demonic Magician before the end of April. I am not fully there but I am pushing along. I will continue. I understand I am chosen to do something, and I just do it now because I'm there. I am not a lackey of any Demon, and I know they have something up their sleeves, because they have a purpose for me. Everything they have asked me to do so far has been for my greater good of an improvement, an enlightenment, and when I do not resist, my growth is not painful. It is beautiful.

I've lost my twin soul and life partner. I miss him terribly. He was my best friend. He motivated and supported me on every level. We met under hard conditions. We fell in love again in this lifetime and we are perfect together, but situations and my behavior and his behavior were not the best and we needed time apart. I've learned my lesson but until he can grow and learn his lesson, we can't be together. If, and when, he does, I'm ready; and if he doesn't, I'm ready to move on. It doesn't mean I don't love him. It means I must love myself and fill my needs. If he can put me on a shelf, I must put him on the shelf because my needs must come first. I must be the anchor in the storm, and I understand completely now that's why Satan gave me my name—the eye of the storm—because I am everybody's anchor not just J's, not just mine, but everybody comes to me to fix things and that has to be my priority. It's not that I'm not capable of love, and it's not that I'm not worthy of love or being loved.

I have so much love that I can't give it to just one person. I am worthy of being loved, and he gave me a lot of love. My fears got in the way and wounded him, and he must heal that. I believe we will be together. It might not be this life and that's OK too. I sent him so much love and healing and the flames of all the candles joined up and united. That was enough for me to know: he is ok, and I am ok, and whatever is going to be? I fixed what I screwed up in the universe. Lucifuge Rofocale is pleased and has now passed me on to be enlightened by Lucifer.

What I do not fully understand is why they all tease me about questions during rituals. I do ask them. But I ask specific, targeted questions about me, and about what I need to do. They tease me, asking if I do not have profound life-altering universal questions. I suppose I am neither deep nor profound. Maybe I am simply goal-driven at the moment. My stock answer for now is if you want to tell me you will. For now? You are in me and if you know it, I should know it, right?

So it shall be, so may it be. So will it be. Thank you.

***

The realization that hit me as I left my altar room was staggering. My job as a healer working with these Demons is like these Demons. My clients, even J, they need me, like we all need the Demons to do the path work, to do the healing. Once we are healed? There is no guarantee they, and in J's case, he, will be back. Sometimes as a healer, our job is to catch, heal, and release and to give our person the tools to move on without us, just like the Demons we utilize in our work. It can be a lonely life these Demons have. It is a fear I have being immersed in this life, as a healer; am I to always heal and never have a true, lasting love for myself? I keep being told J is my forever love by every Gatekeeper, but no one is doing anything to get him off his high horse and bring him back from his own place of confusion. I had to shake that moroseness off and give it to the Gatekeepers, for it has no place in my heart. I am on a mission.

Chapter 7
The Puzzle Pieces Start to Fit Together Snugly

Lucifer, THE Enlightened one, with the venomous Breath.
Oh, how I love thee.

My time with this demon was profound to say the least. For those of you who are new to Demonic Magick, my name is derived from Lucifer, the Bringer of Light, the Enlightened one and Belial, the Lawless one—a combination of the two. LuciaBelia. I am a part of all the Gatekeepers, yet I am enlightened. I can be lawless, and that was the Magick name given to me when I started this journey. The connection with this Demonic Majesty is deep.

During my time with Lucifer, I learned key magical practices. I learned key components of Magick; while summoning him I was told to only call him Lucifer, and I learned a secret I cannot reveal.

I was sitting at my altar with Lucifer, contemplating the dark and the light. Lucifer asked me what I thought of the darkness. I told him it was beautiful, and darkly bright. He laughed. He told me to breathe it in, as did Belial. I told him I always felt safe in the dark and would never need light in the dark to walk around, not even in strange places, because I instinctually found my way. I realized he was hitting me with profound knowledge about myself, not just about the mundane fact that I have bat sonar skills. I always find my way. I can get out of the dark because without darkness we can have no light. We are the way. We are the darkness we bring on our journey of life, and we also may shine the light onto our travels, troubles, and joys.

Lucifer asked me if I had any profound questions for him during our time. I wanted to know the next step in my journey with the Gatekeepers, what was expected of me. I laughed because I replied, "Yes, when will you give me J back?" He roared with delight. He responded with a quick clap of his hands and his head unhinged fully backwards almost robotically.

He said, "LuciaBelia, my dear sweet child, most make pacts to bring new people into their lives, soulmates, people they have never met new, new, new. Why do you want old, old, old? Can you tell me how many lives you have experienced with this man? Have you nothing PROFOUND to ask me about the existential existence of man? Or what lives on Uranus? Anything, dear, sweet LuciaBelia? Your mentor comes to me to trap me with profound questions of who I am, the many faces of Lucifer and you want to know when J will be returned to you and where you will put your left foot or your right foot? How exquisite are you? Have you no fear of me, no shame?"

I leaned in and whispered, "I have no fear, for you shed me of such silly things, dear Lucifer. If you are in me and I am a part of you, I should know all and be all. What I do not know you will tell me when it is time, so why waste my breath with such questions? I suppose I am not as profound as my mentor and all the adepts and masters before me as my purpose is not to answer life's questions of existence, dear Lucifer, but to heal, to be, and to guide—and to be the eye of the storm. I am not here to fulfill your need to explain the purpose of existence, nor am I to be one to ponder the past. As to J and I and our pasts? I only know of two lives."

He laughed and said, "Go to the one who can review it and tell me your last three lives and what you did in those lives. You will find him an active part of all three. If you still want him in this one? You can make it happen when all the riddles have been answered."

I smirked the biggest smirk of my patron Asmodeus and stated, "I was a healer in all. I am sure because for two lives, it is what I did, as J was a warrior and my husband in both."

He looked annoyed and said, "Then go to the third, and if it is so, may it be for this. In the meantime since you solved my riddle as adeptly as you have, you may breathe in my venomous breath as a reward. Your death and rebirth is a rapid rise, dear LuciaBelia. When you speak to Archealus tell him and confront his lie. Do not show fear. Tell him I said to never and see what he says. He will be chagrined and proud like a dad. You truly are the few at the table of many. Do not be hurt if you are not at his table in the end but at ours instead. You have nothing to prove to him. He is your mentor, not your King. Breathe me in, LuciaBelia, and feast at this table today. You have earned that right. I am proud of you. Bring me your answer and you are one more step closer to J, and three steps closer to your empire."

He further asked me to name the first shape that came to me. I said trapezoid, as it is my favorite shape. He laughed because

I suppose I should have said "Death Star," or "pentagram," like a good Satanist, but I am me, and I am not a people pleaser. He told me that I see things in trapezoids and that I am a trapezoid, not the typical pentagram most used as the symbol of Satanism. I had to go look that up and was surprised that the trapezoid is a satanic symbol of reunion. Huh. Go Lucifer, you sneaky bastard, shooting knowledge into me, yet again.

You are being turned over to Ba'al now.

Chapter 8
Creating Connections, Spaces, and Kingdoms

Beautiful, sweet Ba'al, King of Kings, Lord of Lords: one of the most misunderstood, in my humble opinion. He is a mover and a shaker of the Demons, and he makes things happen if you only listen and learn.

Ba'al is about connections. He wants us to be our best selves. Working with Ba'al was a pure joy. I had already started making connections. Reaching out to people and making friends. I thought, *yup, Ba'al won't want to do much.* I was proud, hey—I made friends; I had done my homework; I was taking classes; I had met some LHP women. I was moving. Shaking. Doing BIG THINGS. I HAD PLANS FOR MY EMPIRE!

Ok, so I am beyond stupid for my 147 IQ. Ba'al started our meditation with a "Good morning, LuciaBelia. Sorry to disturb your lie-in." It was 2:45 a.m. I was about to get a demonic boot camp with this demon of my own. I knew it was time to add the death coffee to my Nespresso black before I showered. This was Death Con 5:00 a.m. brew time.

My meditation with Ba'al was not the typical meditation. I was not called to scry. I was not channeled. I was possessed. I had been possessed before. This King of Kings had a mission, and it was important. He wanted me to see my Kingdom, my Empire, my Vision, from his eyes.

Do not give up LuciaBelia, not for a second! Push past the barriers, the boundaries holding you back. When you think you are there? You are simply on the step to success. RISE UP, RISE UP, RISE MY CHILD! Wake up and move!

Your Kingdom, your Empire of Infernal Darkness is being built but you can make it so much more. You must build it to a higher level. You are capable of more. THINK BIGGER. Close your eyes and picture each puzzle piece the previous Gatekeeper has given you and lay it out in that raven's mind of yours. Put it together like the road map it is. Fit them together and walk your path. The road is paved with a beautiful, dark path laid out in front of you. Do not allow them to lead you with a string of what is next. Demand your answers. You are special. Everyone feels they are the next great thing. You have a purpose, and you are special. I say this only to a few, ask your mentor if you do not believe me.

Let me help you my sweet, beautiful Queen.

1. *Satan's eye, the anchor*

2. *The desert and crossroads looping back, flames of fire and lightning*

3. *Facing fears, geometric shapes, trapezoids, healing gifts*

4. *Lucifer and his name, breathing in his venomous breath, accepting the darkness is light itself*

5. *Understanding Lucifuge Rofocale is spiritual, the emotions brought on during rituals must be harnessed as energy for potency. It is ok to disengage the trauma to heal it, not to engage and relive it. The candle flames show three layers. The number "3" has significance and while three meditations of each Gatekeeper, three parts to each riddle, there is only one right answer to each.*

6. *Making connections, building kingdoms. Defining my purpose and locking the puzzle pieces together, understanding my Godhood allows me to stand up to what is in my way. Ba'al made me define who I am and where I was going. The Demonic Powers within guide me, the Gatekeepers have a path and plan, but I determine what I am doing.*

7. *Lord of Flies, relationships, relativity, lifetimes, defining my personal purpose, as a person, as a lover, as a woman, as a queen. Without a direction, where do I step?*

8. *Finding my balance and power between love and anger, death, and destruction. Why do I fear destruction and anger?*

9. *The abyss, fall into the darkness, let go vs. let's go. Burn Azazel and his studies to the ground, not the literal Azazel to the ground.*

*He continued to tell me that I needed to take an imaginary carton of eggs and take two out. That was the origin of the new, he said. "The New Beginning of Time." The laying of the new plan being hatched. **The Revolution of Revivre**. Ten people come together to form this from different disciples: some of my choosing, some my mentor would call on. The new revolution of awakening. The trusted trapezoid of the reborn, born from my marketing plan and developed within weeks. Created from lifetimes of dedication: blood, sweat, and tears. A journey of beginnings and starts and stops but when one struggles, many make light work.*

What is my purpose versus my priority? Death, rebirth, victory: it comes at a cost you must be willing to take. Who is LuciaBelia? Pick a face. You have many—not from deception—from necessity, protection, and trauma. PUSH FUCKING THROUGH MY GENIUS!

I thought that reaching out to the women in the LHP was a great effort. It was only a drop in the bucket. I was working hard with the Gatekeepers. I was writing the Eastern Star Rising book. I was mentoring. I had my reading, life coaching, and boot camp clients through Satan's Eye Of The Storm. I was studying the Blackwitchcoven.com demonology course. I had literally just finished my iNLP hypnotherapy course. I was looking to start radionics certification. I was doing a month-long Mammon Altar. I was doing daily invocations, evocations . . . I was filling my supplies up. I was up by 3:00 a.m. and in bed by 9:00 p.m. I had a young lady I was mentoring who is like a daughter to me. I literally had no life.

When did I do these extra things? Well, I meditated on it, and I figured it out because Demonic Magick is not something I find the time for. It is me. It is an extension of me, and this is my life.

If Ba'al says, "Make fucking connections," I make connections. I was told that I needed four mentors. WTF? What is wrong with E.A.? HAHA. "Nothing," Ba'al says. He is a king of kings in his kingdom of the Eternal Flame. But I need more. Find four. "Figure it out," I am told. Ok. I will figure it out. Nothing more than that, thanks, Ba'al. These Demons help, they really do, but they will not ever spoon-feed you. The work is up to you.

***

I have forged an amazing friendship—no, brotherhood—with 777 of ClaviculaNoxBoutique in New Mexico. I trust him with my life; this amazing, kind, gentle, loving soul of a necromancing genius. He will move mountains for those in his circle and I feel blessed to be in his circle. I do not know what I have done to be blessed with his admission, but I will fight to keep it, and fight to protect him even though he is capable of greatness and protection of his own right. Satan help anyone who messes with my kid brother, is all I have to say. If you need any work, any tools, any altar supplies? Go to ClaviculaNoxBoutique. com on Etsy. 777 is by far an expert on all things he speaks of. If he does not know? He is genuine enough to say that he does not know and gallant enough to go and look. I have bullied this quiet, loving, and kind man into coming to the LHP Convention as well because I know he must be there (for reasons that are not mine to share). Their paths must cross. I am so glad that we will be sharing that time and cannot wait until he and his wife will be my guests up here in the mountains of Maine.

I have met an amazing woodcarver in the Netherlands named Razvan who hears my thoughts and creates my visions into genius creations and unique designs and ships them to me faster than artists here in America. We have forged a friendship I cherish, and I wish he were closer so we could share a cup of coffee and a meal occasionally. He is truly an artist and a soul I cherish spending time with. He is a man I respect who respects his art. His work adorns my altar and my home with pride of place, just like 777. These two men and their art are an extension of their spiritual selves, and it reflects in their art. You cannot ask for more.

***

Ba'al has pushed me to get a marketing plan done. I realized I am more than capable of doing it myself, but I do not have the time. I started the journey to hire a marketing expert. I went through fourteen companies. Some allowed me to book, some even took payments of up to $1,400, and my valuable time in the process, only to cancel and or refund my money telling me my ethos did not align with them and they did not want to work with me.

I laughed because I was not even promoting Magick in my marketing plan, simply the hypnotherapy, life coaching, and healing aspects. I refused to change my company name as one website suggested; they took my time for an appointment but never bothered to call me back.

One company took an hour of my time—DSL, Digital Software Labs—had me sign the contract, took my $1,400, had me fill out endless questionnaires for them to do my marketing and social media, only to tell me via email the following day in the rudest and most cowardly way they were refunding my money and they were not going to work with me because . . . gasp! I was a Satanist! By the way, I was upfront with this detail and mentioned it straightaway. I was even sent an email rudely and quite unprofessionally telling me that the person who signed this contract was fired. As if I would do business with a company who airs their dirty laundry in such a way? Yet, I am considered the lowlife? Please, people. Look at yourselves and ask who aligns with whom here.

We all do business. Those fourteen companies who refused to do a simple business transaction are all hypocrites. They refused because what? I am a Satanist? Because they do not believe in hypnosis? It's unclear.

Regardless, I persevered and found a guy in India. He seemed willing. Sounded like he knew what he was doing. I hired him. I am not going to say his name. The following day, I came across BrandedAlex1 on Fiverr. Yes, Fiverr. I knew he was the one and I hired him on the spot for the highest tier he had. He is in Germany. I loved his energy; I loved his vibe. He completely got my vision and there was no issue with what I was doing and that was awesome. Being a psychic has its perks. The guy from India asked for an extension of three days. I gave it. I knew he was not going to deliver. I did not care, I had Alex. I was secure. Sure enough the delivery date came and no delivery; there was never any communication from the gentleman from India. When I went to Resolution Center to cancel, he was given two days. Originally, he refused, asking for another extension. He asked for another extension saying there were festivals going on and he needed more time because he was partying. I do not care if it was Ramadan, Christmas, the most holy of holy days on Earth. Business is business and an obligation is an obligation. I refused. I resubmitted and was given a credit on Fiverr. Was I a bitch for this? I do not care. I take on a client and I do my job. I do not say once I take a payment, "Sorry, I was partying I am going to be late." It is funny because as a Satanist, we are evil and no one wants to work with us, yet it appears I have more morals and ethics than most who I have worked with on marketing.

Another woman on Fiverr yelled at me for booking an order without speaking to her first and cancelled my order because she did not like me. She did not know me. She simply was a Christian spouting hate. I pity these people who cannot separate their work and personal life, who think they are right and who cannot simply separate, "I do my job when it comes to work." I do not ask my clients their beliefs; I put mine out there because it is how I heal. I have a spectrum of people who come to me: from the hypocrite Judeo-Christian wanting a ritual done who will go to mass and pray for forgiveness to the Muslim to the LHP. I do not judge. I do my job. Ok, I do judge. I call them hypocrites because they are; they are the ones who want Magick to work and question when it does not.

***

Demonick Magick is an art form. It is a ritual, a mass of a form, performed to create a shift in energy to bend. You must believe in it. You must participate in it. You must ask for it, do what is asked, then let it go into the universe. Those who hover, those who doubt, those who constantly ask a pendulum or tarot, "Is it happening today?" or go to multiple practitioners? You won't get far in the Magickal Realm. It is Magickal. But there is work you must do as well. Magick is reciprocal, offerings are made. I could go on, but that is for another chapter.

I realized I needed three more mentors and Ba'al wanted me to find them. I watched the Deification ritual performed by E.A. Koetting, Andrieh Vitimus, Martin McGreggor, and ND Blackwell.

Andrieh had sent me a sigil previously right after the ritual with Nix. He channeled for me to work with Nix. I knew I needed to work with Nix. I thought, *well, we are both iNLP Practitioners and he is highly trained;* but no, he is not to be my mentor.

The next video was Martin McGreggor. As soon as the video started, I knew I had to reach out to this humble Satanist who used the Grigori Runes. He channeled Baraquiel for me, The Watcher, The Fallen Angel of Fire, Lightning. During my time practicing Santeria, I have been given by a high-ranking Santero, OYA, the Mother of Storms. I channel storms. I can bring them on when I am in a rage. I feel calm in a storm as well, so it was fitting and true for him to pull this. I knew he was supposed to be my mentor.

I reached out. He was rapid and humble with a response, and we consulted the following day. I felt a deep connection and knew I was right. I will not yet discuss our mentoring in detail; however, Martin is by far in line with my beliefs on where Satanism and the LHP needs to go. He is one of the most calm and humble men I have met, right up there with the Right Reverend Bill Duvendack and E.A. Koetting. People laugh when I say E.A. is humble. If you do not think that he is, you truly do not know this man.

I set up weekly sessions to learn what this mammoth brain of Satanic knowledge can teach me, and I am extremely excited of where it is going to lead me. I want to become learned on the Grigori and on his wealth of actual knowledge on Satanism itself because we cannot press forward and push mainstream if we are not aware of what and where we came from. We cannot set the example of Satanism publicly if we ourselves are not genuine to our crafts. Martin sits in himself, and it shines out like a beacon. A sign for sure.

My next mentor I tackled was the Right Reverend Bill Duvendack. I have been working with him on my Demonic birth chart, tarot readings, my pact with Lucifuge, and a few other things here and there. But it was time to nail him down for weekly sessions. Nail him down. The battle with Right Reverend Bill Duvendack is not that he does not want to impart his wisdom. He is generous with his time and knowledge as well as being extremely funny, witty, and clever. I find each one of these men share a part of my personality to an extent.

The problem with the Right Reverend Bill Duvendack I have is financial. Getting him to agree to a price was tricky. The same thing happened with Martin, who generously offered me a discount. I declined. These men, who know their worth, do not charge enough. I refused Martin's price and sent him what I felt his time was worth. It is a personal thing to me, stemming from knowing my worth and refusing to pay a mentor less than what I would take, and not wanting to cheat someone of their time and generosity. It also comes from knowing they are in my life to teach me wisdom. I am in theirs to teach them their worth. An hour of someone's years of experience and wisdom should not cost dimes. It is well worth the cost of a dinner and movie night out. I believe this with my whole heart, and I will get him to raise his prices. Knowledge is power. We will pay $10 for a pack of cigarettes. I do not get questioned on my rates. People pay it or they do not. Simple as that. My head is on straight, and I know my worth. There is no room in my energy for argument, so I get none.

I received my consultation and we agreed to do mentoring. I think he simply knew at this point that I was going to PayPal him whatever I wanted to pay so he did not argue. I love this man. He is devilishly lovely, sarcastic, and valid: things I cherish, and aspects of me.

During our chat we discussed the fourth mentor. I was tossing out names and we were both no'ing them as soon as they came out. I was told no women because I have a masculine-leaning energy and I would destroy a feminine energy. Too much envy, or jealousy, I do not know exactly, but I accepted the demonic ruling because I had wanted Asenath as a mentor. Demonic Powers said not right now.

Bill cunningly asked if it needed to be human. We stared at each other in dawning awe because I got simultaneously, "No, it does not, dumbass; it is about damn time. The fourth mentor is to be Choronzon." More importantly, without Bill and his tutelage, I would not ever have found that one on my own.

Puzzle pieces slip into place that fit on the periphery not given by the demons. People in your life often have key roles, so take nothing for granted. I have a Grimoire for Magick. I have a daily journal for my time tracking. I have notes for things that strike me. I have a five-ringed binder filled with graph paper close by my laptop. I am old school. I handwrite my notes. My book is handwritten into the journal before I type it out. I like to breathe it in and feel it come out of me onto paper before it comes off my fingertips and onto the screen.

My time with Ba'al ended with a lot of flies in a large sunroom during a blizzard so severe that it shut down the airport for the day. My client coming for boot camp got turned around at Washington Dulles and sent back to Florida. I knew Beelzebub was coming for a visit.

Chapter 9
Questions, Symbols, and Finding the Answers

Prince of Devils. Lord of Flies. I know his presence each and every time. How do you ask? In the middle of a Maine winter, I have black flies in my sunroom. He is here and he has things to share. Beelzebub has much to say to me during my time with him. Rather, he has much to do, and he has much for me to do. Beelzebub is a doer. He will not tolerate stagnation. He will question everything you believe to be true. Not because it is wrong—because that is his job. He shakes things loose. I have come to think of him as "the un-doer." I am, in my humble opinion, the queen of sitting in my thoughts. I can sit and meditate in discipline and dig deep with concentration and focus. Until Beelzebub. He makes you dig deeper.

Have you ever challenged yourself to meditate for an hour without interruption? I'm not talking about a guided meditation where someone is in control, or where there is music, and you can fall asleep and cheat yourself out of healing or resolution. I meditated with Beelzebub. I did the three rites of Beelzebub. I followed my mentor E.A. down into the realm of the unnamed, as I call it, the undoing, rather.

They are E.A.'s to name so I will not go into detail. They can be found in the *Grimoire of Beelzebub* by E.A. Koetting.

1. Baht Rachor takes and gives life

2. Balam Tehor controls thoughts and twists minds

3. Zal'at Saphon reveals all secrets

I then went on to perform the Black Mass of Beelzebub. This is also found in Chapter Four of the Grimoire of Beelzebub. It involves saying a very potent word and an hour-long chant with the sound of Beelzebub: "MMM."

Be forewarned, if you dare to do this, do not stop for anything. Do not dare to fall asleep. Do not even consider looking at your phone. This is critical. Your mind must be clear of all things. You think you are dedicated? Do this ritual meditation with Beelzebub and then come talk to me. If you can do this meditation for an hour? I will applaud you. I did it, and I struggled. It took every muscle in my body to do this and I am humbly saying this. I am not a beginner. I felt like a baby meditator. As E.A. says in his many direct ways, "If you cannot take control of one hour of your life? How are you going to take control of existence?"

I am going to add to that: If you cannot take control of one full hour of your life, how can you manipulate energy for an entire hour when a ritual you must perform requires it? That is what got me through the hour of dedication to Beelzebub without straying.

I then went on to do the Unbaptism. I added and adjusted the Unbaptism to suit my life, and you need to do as you feel fit to do. I followed Beelzebub and his guidance during this time and felt I did what was right for me during this ritual. Beelzebub is an amazing Lord of his own right and has a unique way of constructing deconstruction and rebuilding a better you while you think he is destroying all you know. When he leaves you all you can say is, "Wow, did that just happen? How do I feel so whole and alive?"

Because the entire time he is there it is tests and riddles and challenges about all you believe to be true. If you are not strong enough in your convictions and stand your ground, he will get you to back down. Sometimes you do need to change your opinion, or perspective, but sometimes you do not, and it is a test. You learn to know yourself with Beelzebub; that is the key with him. What came to me and the puzzle piece he brought to me during my meditation was very clear. I always write in my new journal: *What is my purpose?*

Beelzebub wanted to know, "Who is LuciaBelia? What is her purpose? Not the great PR press release you want to sell yourself as. What is your purpose for yourself?"

What is your purpose for others? Who are you to yourself? Who are you for others?

Chapter 10

Finding My Perfect Balance with Asmodeus during Trying Times

Asmodeus, my co-patron. What can you say about this Demon? I started my LHP calling Asmodeus, using Ars Goetia Sigil Magic, sleeping with his sigil under my pillow as many suggest to manifest dreams. I invoked him back in October 2022. He came to me in several visions in different forms: as a handsome man, dressed charmingly, willingly partaking in my Knappogue Castle twenty-one-year-old Irish whiskey gifted to me, and espousing wisdom about my situation at the time.

I was new to the LHP but not new to Magick and knew instinctually this was one slippery fucker. I was fascinated by his eloquence, and his tales of history; knowledge of Magick; and his knowledge of J. His full understanding and comprehension of what was going on was equivalent to Tzu's *Art of War*. I fell in love with his intelligence, not in love with the Demonic Lord, with his mind. As the days passed, he started to get stepped on by Satan. It began to dawn on me that he was sent to deliver messages to me and had a purpose, not to simply wax poetic.

I had to laugh. Satan was not pleased with the whiskey-swilling, time-wasting Asmodeus. Asmodeus was not exactly pleased with the interruptions either because his form started to come differently, impatiently.

You have to know this demonic genius. If you do not, you will get toyed with. With liar's lips he will introduce himself as another's name. He does this for many reasons. You need to know what you are doing when you are working with Demonic Magick. It is not a game. It is an art form. I do not, as I have said before, practice it. It is an extension of myself. The quote, "If you cut me, do I not bleed . . . ?" If a demon appears, I know it, and I know who it is. They cannot fool me. A fly appears, it may simply be a fly. Several flies appear. I will tell people, "Ahhh, Beelzebub is here." I sense their energy. Nothing gets past me, and Asmodeus tested me, and he failed. Many times. But if you do ask, "Are you Asmodeus?" he must be honest with you. Simply put, he can try to fool you to test your integrity and your skill, but he cannot lie.

As my meditation and education with Asmodeus deepened and his smirks continued, I started not to trust him—not because he was dishonest, but because deep beneath his surface lay a depth of wrath and rage that I completely identified with, a destruction so complete and satisfying that I lay buried and feared and did not want to touch just yet. I even avoided Asmodeus to an extent. I even mistrusted his love and lust. I was going through a painful separation of my twin soul, and nothing was bringing him back. What good was Asmodeus to me if he could not snap his fingers with his many legions and make things happen? Right? That smirk made me doubt because what I saw in Asmodeus was a mirror in my face and it reflected the depth of my soul. I was not ready to admit. That was the Asmodeus puzzle. What is your deepest darkest secret you hide from the world, LuciaBelia?

It took the Gatekeepers' Ritual for me to come to terms with the fact that I am Satan's Eye of the Storm. That also means that I am chaos. I am surface. I am layers and I am death, destruction, love, wrath, lust, and seduction. I am the queen of my kingdom in perfect unison and what I feared most was what I saw in my mirror every single day. By admitting this about myself I no longer feared it, because what you admit, what you face, what you fear and shine the darkest, brightest light on cannot harm you or anyone else because it no longer controls you. You control it. I realized while I was shoving these beautiful things about me down, not unleashing the fury and rage when necessary, I was actually giving my power away to others and allowing them control over me. I was not powerful; I was the powderpuff queen submitting and rolling over, walking away, afraid to blow up, and not give reactions because I feared blowing up.

The reality was that I was a calm person, and I could decide when to react. If I felt justified in exploding, then it was ok to explode. When I do explode, I have been told it is beautiful to behold and to not hold back. I can bring on a storm when I explode. I have made a sunny day rain and I have brought on storm clouds, with pelting hard rain. That has brought me joy in a perverse way and my Santeria guardian has made me go out and dance in it. My Irish druid past has made me, in fury, go out and scream like a banshee in rage and cast salt into the screeching wind as I screamed my rage and angst and curse at whomever had brought it out, getting drenched in the storm. Relieving the rage. Cathartic. Once spent, the storm has passed.

I have also healed people in the center of these passing storms, bringing love and passion and reuniting lost loves while gale force winds pass by me. I am oblivious to their existence with Asmodeus's tutelage. As I have said, I am the conduit, and I can determine how I heal. I determine how I heal myself, how I heal the client, how I heal the world. We live taking one step in front of the other. Asmodeus in his ever-charming, ever-clever, brilliant, smirking awe-inspiring way has shown me that you cannot have healing without destruction and love, lust without fury, and rage is boring. Everything in life has a time and place. It is ok to mix it up and it is ok to separate it all.

Asmodeus is one of the most underrated and over-abused Demons of the Gatekeepers. I am blessed to have him as a co-patron, and I am grateful he pushed forward and stepped up to be my patron. Much gets done at Casa LuciaBelia because he gets the job done. So it shall be, so it is, and so it is, and so it is again, and again, and again, in perfect harmony.

Chapter 11

Finding the Light at the Bottom of the Black Abyss

Abaddon, Lord of the Abyss, the Dark Lord of Destruction. I lived in fear of this Lord. Why, do you ask? Because during my Gatekeepers' ritual he did not come forth. He did not offer to be a patron. Vanity, my name is LuciaBelia, right? No, that is not the only reason.

He, during all my meditations with the Gatekeepers, eyed me in my self-judgment perspective state, looking deep into my soul. He saw me on a deeper level than anyone or anything ever had before.

I show many faces to the world; not fake or phony at all. I am an honest person, what you see is what you get. However, I am extremely private, and I show surface. I am "an onion," someone once said. Depending on who you are, you get what I give you. Because of my gifts, I listen, I absorb everything around me, and people feel close to me. However, I do not always feel close to them. It is not their fault; my core onion is deep, and I only share it with a select few. I am genuine with every person I encounter, but they only get layers of me. The many facets of me I show: I am woman, I am healer, I am lover, I am rage, I am calm, I am destruction, I am smart, I am strength, I am wisdom, I am the keys, I am the lock, I am the gate. I am the path, the light, and the way. I am chaos and the calm before the storm. I am the conduit that can lead you into the storm or around the storm into the better version of yourself and I decide.

His statement during the Gatekeepers' Ritual was that I did not ask for enough. That floored me because of statements made against me in my past. I had learned to ask for little. I received much because I worked hard, but I asked for little.

Abaddon made me stop and think while making my pact with Lucifuge. "Why do I ask for so LITTLE?"

Yes, LITTLE, in capital letters because Little is a noun when it comes to abundance and manifesting and what we deserve. Why did I refuse to set my worth where I set my work? Abaddon, Lord of Destruction, had struck a chord deep within my psyche well before he started working with me. Food to ponder on. The little girl with the eating disorder needed time to digest this and he knew I would kick that around in the nether regions of my subconscious brain, and when it was his term to deconstruct and rebuild, I would be ready to go for broke and be a Queen of Darkness.

I had fallen willingly into the Abyss back in November, proudly backwards, freely knowing what I was doing, changing my life around. Forging new friendships and alliances, creating. Abaddon knew this but he wanted me to not simply fall. He wanted me to fly. Reminding me of my four-year-old Wonder Woman self, leaping freely off that slide. I started to flash back to that day and realized it was not one or two of these Demonic Lords present but all of them, the Watchers, their Legions, the Fallen, poised to take over, had something terribly gone awry. It dawned on me that I was chosen for a path extremely special, and I was expected to pull this off with poise and dignity and without failure.

I looked Abaddon in the eyes and asked, "What is next? I am no longer afraid of you, Lord Abaddon." He asked me to put my arms out and simply be willing to fall at a moment's notice when he asked. He asked me to be willing to continue to let go and know that by letting go I was dying and preparing for my rebirth. He asked me how much I trusted the Demons, and my mentors. I did not hesitate when I answered with my life because it was truthful. I was not even surprised at the answer. I instinctively knew that E.A. had become my family; whether he knew it yet or not was irrelevant. The level of trust in him was on par with J: the two men I trusted with my life in this world. It hit me in the face that list had multiplied because 777 of ClaviculaNoxBoutique was now on that list, as was Right Reverend Bill Duvendack, and Martin McGreggor. I breathed in deeply and said, "Let's go, Abaddon. What do you have in store for me?"

He put his hand in front of my face and stated: "All that you once knew is going to be gone, and what you will begin to know will be exponential, LuciaBelia. Your hard work, your gifts, your faith, everything you have done, gone. Up in flames and smoke and down into the abyss all simultaneously. You are about to be destroyed by Archelaus, and you will willingly allow him to kill you. You are not your brother's keeper, nor is he yours. But your brother is about to cast a death spell on you that would render a weaker person dead. Are you ready?"

I answered yes. I knew what he was referring to because E.A. was going to finish off my Gatekeepers' Challenge with a ritual for Abaddon that Tuesday. I was simply not aware of how literal this Dark Lord was being.

***

On the Tuesday following my meditation, I started getting dizzy and alarm bells were raging inside my head. I am extremely and demonically protected as an adept/Master. If you are not granted permission to be in my energy, or if you think you are clever enough to try to cast a hex, curse, or spells on me without my knowledge, think again. I feel it before it hits me, that is how gifted I am. I immediately emailed E.A. and asked if he had started the ritual because it simply did not feel right at all. I was messaging Sara from Blacktreeblueraven and when she asked if it was from anticipation of the ritual, we both said nope, not at all. I started to cook and keep busy but instantly rejected and returned whatever paltry bs white magic was trying to invade my space back to who it came from; I was able to determine who sent it, I am that good. I laughed at her for trying. Is she that desperate for J? Oh sweetie, you will not win that battle, not ever. You cannot keep twin souls apart forever, sorry. Not even the black demonic Magick she has hired to betray him has worked because he fights it. He contacts me; sometimes love is stronger than will and might. I have not interfered with her and him yet because I do not want to take his free will away and I fully accept the depth and breadth of our soul connection and know that the Gatekeepers have a plan for us. Her trying to send me harm? Well, I am the storm, so she needs to worry about that one once this challenge is over. We in the LHP do not tend to turn the other cheek and I have a lot of rage building within me over her bad character and abuse over J. Her trying to hex and curse me doesn't bode well for her.

I sensed E.A. in my aura energy and let go. I later received an email from him outlining the Abaddon ritual and was told it was a full stop because he was going to do a complete DEATH/ DESTRUCTION ritual per Abaddon. This is not a joke. I teased and said how dramatic he was. But this was not a joke. This is a ritual performed within Satanism when you want someone dead. Abaddon had instructed E.A. to perform the death ritual on me with full Enochian Keys. E.A. had repeated back to him something along the line of, "It will kill her."

The response was, "If it were anyone other than LuciaBelia, yes, yes it would. However, she will die and rise back up. She will come through this because she is strong."

We did the ritual the following day. E.A. had sensed something wrong before he heard from me stating something was wrong. He had projected to me, saw me cooking, felt all was well, then was guided to read emails. He read the email but proceeded with caution and postponed the ritual until Wednesday.

***

I knew as soon as E.A. had started the ritual. I was on the phone with a client discussing a ritual I would be performing for him and had to excuse myself and call him back three times. I was sick and vomiting. I laughed, I was luckily close to this client, and he knew what was happening. I had to go and take a bubble bath, something I normally do not do, especially during an eighteen-hour day for me. I felt like I was dying. I was both grateful E.A. did not give me a heads up it was being done, and annoyed because had I been driving, I may have crashed. I had to tell Abaddon, "Some notice, asshole?" He roared with delight and said, "Suck it up, Lucia, and soak in the darkness." I remember not much else for about fifteen minutes.

When E.A. finished and sent me the video, I watched it. Tears formed because he was so apprehensive doing this ritual, it was apparent. He did it and was amazing doing it, but you could see, he knew he was calling forth my actual death. The trust and faith he had in Abaddon in his faith was pure. To resurrect me. I was in agony in my abdomen watching the video of the ritual. I have had a lot of abdominal surgeries and had the rite of unction in my Catholic past because I was not going to make it through the night in 2007. I survived that. I was in the ICU for eight weeks, but I pulled through.

I survived the ritual. My life did flash as a movie screen during this ritual. I realized Abaddon was killing the old me, the broken me, the abused me, the human me, the pieces of me, the mundane me. He was resurrecting LuciaBelia, the Magickal me, the perfect and whole me, the me who is meant to be. The me who has learned, the me who is healed, the me who falls and flies. The me who is in the Gatekeepers and who has the Gatekeepers within.

LuciaBelia survived but only because her brother, Archelaus, killed her to rise again. The Phenix from the ashes rises incandescent: healing, guiding, knowing, sensing, and seeing what to do, where to go, and how to get there. Her path is lit with knowledge instilled by death and resurrection by falling into an abyss of darkened light. A frozen space of time that is expansive, constantly moving, and beating to a sound only the few sitting at the table of the many can hear. The Dragon's Egg sitting on the secret trapezoid being watched by the fallen who know how to that to fly you must fall. That know basic geometry is 2x2, 3x3x3x3x3, is 5x5x5x5x5, is LHP, Satanism, Luciferianism, Necromancy, Vampirism. Black Magick and all that is in between. Both siblings will choose who sits at that table and the network will be formed. The masks are set, and the future is unfolding. Recognize that to lead you must lay your fears at the bottom of the abyss and know it is time, so it is time, so may it be, so will it be. So, it is.

Chapter 12
The Mental Athletics That We Call Mentoring

Mentoring has been challenging. During a meditation it was channeled to get four mentors, all males. I was extremely confused because I was working weekly with E.A. and that was in and of itself a handful. Homework, ritual work he was doing, ritual work I was doing, invocation, evocations, a possession or two, writing this book, studying the Ars Goetia, researching the LHP in general, and working with my own clientele was a full workload. I was already investing over ninety full hours a week minimally. I was doing a monthly altar to Lord Mammon. I was working with a few Demons intimately. I was unsure how to fulfill this request. I knew I was not going to refuse this because I realized it was not a request: it was with purpose for my path, and my greater good. I set out to fulfill this, keeping my ears and eyes open to the possibilities of who would be my best fit. I have touched on this previously, but this is the breakdown.

Working with mentors is a fine balance. Especially in Satanism. The Left Hand Path is not an easy path to follow, especially after so many years of being what I have been. In many ways, I have acclimated rapidly because I did not have a clear path. I followed the beat of my own drum, using customs and rituals and learning pieces of paths of different spiritual systems that fit me, incorporating them into me. I used Santeria, and found a guardian in Oya, my Mother Protectress. I have gained immense knowledge and counsel from Salvadore Gata over the years, not to mention immense healing in the art of Santeria. He is one of the most prolific Santeros I have ever met, and if you ever get to LA and his Botanica, he is a first-come-first-serve-put-your-name-on-the-list-and-wait Botanica type of guy. I suggest you sign up the night before in Echo Park and wait because the list starts at 9:00 or 10:00 p.m. the night before he opens. He closes shop the next day when he is finished, so it may not be until 2:00 a.m. when the last client is complete. You will not regret your choice; his consultation is worth it, and any cleanse performed is transformational.

I used Voodoo and Hoodoo. Many mistakenly believe they are one and the same, but trust me, they are vastly different spiritual systems. Hoodoo is an amazing root working system. As a healer, I have employed Hoodoo great deal. I have followed the wisdom and teachings of Angelie Belard and her books and found them profound. I, to this day, use root work in my distance healing practice and in ritual work. Without that knowledge, I would be, frankly, at a loss in many ways.

I lovingly and respectfully work with Santa Muerte and have an altar for her set up in a private room. Without Holy Death, I would feel empty. She will be my next tattoo for all she gives me in protection, healing, peace, and joy.

I worked in the past with the Old Ones and studied them to the limited ability many have with limited knowledge available. I had to go with the books available and the rest was my own meditation and work with them and what came with utilizing that work was what I chose to incorporate. I still often go back to the Old Ones occasionally because I do not throw anything I learn away.

My time spent overseas for so many years allowed me the luxury many do not get. I was able to meditate in actual faery rings in Belfast. I was able to sit on the St. Charles Bridge in Prague and breathe in the air and close my eyes and envision claircognizant thoughts that spirit had led me there to feel and see and sense. I often do what I am led to do because I know when I feel or sense something not to argue. I do it with purpose and I do not resist.

In the same vein, I was drawn to many negative places as well, to experience both sides of humanity. As a healer we must see both good and evil and know it to heal it. Shadow work is based on this. It is knowing ourselves and our dark side that allows us to see it in others. One of those trips was a concentration camp outside of Prague on the Poland border.

**

When I decided to go LHP, and specifically Theistic Satanism, it was not a choice I took lightly, but it was one I took readily and rapidly. Many people may look at my journey and say, "She put no thought into it." Or, "She is in a hurry and pushes through it without investing the time."

Here are my responses: "I am doing my pace with which I am comfortable. My rise within the LHP, my mastery, is a personal journey and it is guided specifically by the Gatekeepers." And, "I owe nobody an explanation; I owe myself the journey. I owe myself the lessons that come with learning this journey and to not cheat myself of the powerful blessings that come with learning this amazing spiritual system that is Satanism and all the positives and negatives that come out of it."

I am also going to say, I chose this path willingly, but the path chose me. I have a purpose within the LHP that supersedes even me, my business, my clients, and my personal growth comes with this purpose as I grow the purpose grows. A lot changed for me in the last week of Gatekeepers' work. I am going to try to define it, and how it ties in with what I believe needs to happen next.

***

During my mentorship with E.A., he has done several major rituals for me that have been transformational. His consultations have been informative, and grounding for me. Without him, I know I would be lost in the quicksand of time and pressure and quagmire of "red tape" of finding many things that he has willingly and readily helped me with that has put me on a trajectory path to reach the goal that Satan set out for me back in November.

Many people do not like E.A. They take issue with him; they think a lot of things. I laugh a lot at what I see and hear online about him and the few comments I get when they hear he is my mentor. I get a little defensive of him—ok, a lot defensive—protective, like a big sister. E.A. is E.A. He is a large-scale, larger-than-life personality on screen. He is this way because what he has to say is important. It is relevant, and it needs to be heard. I will be fifty-four this year; I have traveled the world; and I can say unequivocally, he is also one of the most humble and honest people I have worked with. He is true to himself. That is rare and it's why I like him. He is talented and he produces results, which many armchair magicians of the LHP cannot. I am not one to say negative things about people, especially publicly, and if I do post something, like, you are an idiot? Trust and believe in the power behind those few words.

About E.A.: he is no one's fool either and he will call you on your bullshit. I like that because I am the same. Many people cannot handle that about my energy. I would like to see more people have an adult conversation, have boundaries be addressed, and real conversations be had and without hard feelings when it is completed and the work proceeds. That would be amazing—real adulting 101 in the LHP.

***

My second mentor is Martin McGreggor. I was really amazed during my Deification Ritual with Become A Living God to watch Martin work. I felt the pressure to find the other mentors Lucifuge and Asmodeus were asking me to find and it hit me while watching that Martin was a perfect choice. When I reached out to him, I saw why.

This man, who is extremely busy with a family, a business, and his own magickal practices was willing to take the time for me and the things that I had addressed that were important.

I had to admit, I had not read his books. Embarrassingly and funnily enough, what I was wanting to do with the path trajectory I was on was absolutely in line with his writing. I was connected because I felt led by the ritual and I wanted to learn the Grigori. Once I started to talk to Martin at length, and realized there was more to this story, I knew my choice was steeped with layers.

Martin is an amazing mentor. His knowledge of Satanism, the LHP, and Demonology is encyclopedic. His integrity about Satanism, and where leadership is in the LHP is admirable. I enjoy our conversations; they leave me asking myself some serious questions weekly when we depart. Since I started working with Martin, I have deepened my understanding of the Grigori; worked deeper with Mammon, whom I was already starting the March Altar for, but branched even further with it; and explored Mulcifer, the Architect into it as I am further growing Satan's Eye Of The Storm into LuciaBelia.com and a practitioners' networking platform: revolutionrevivre. com. These are invaluable time-saving tools which have cataclysmically and exponentially expanded my businesses.

It also made me realize a few things about the LHP that I already knew about surface layers. We are broken in many ways without clear-cut leadership. The LHP, and specifically Satanism, is so fractured that there is no clear guidance, no community— it is a sole practitioner of sense, and as E.A. recently told me, it is "self-initiation." Yes, it is, but people should not go it alone. We have resources. We have leadership. We have knowledge within. Why is it so hidden? Digging deeper with the Gatekeepers in the last few weeks in meditation and removing the veils of onion layers blinding me with the help of my mentors has been eye-opening, to say the least. Martin has a way about him that is knowledgeable, humble, and authoritative. You cannot help but want to be a better person when you are around him. He is truly a leader, and I like to think of him as a champion and preserver to the spiritual system. He does not think short term. He thinks generational preservation and that, to me, has added value.

***

I started to work weekly with the Right Reverend Bill Duvendack as a third mentor. Yes, my week has started to bulge with work and homework.

Working with Bill is different in many ways. Each mentor brings something different to the table. Bill is academic and knowledgeable, as are both Martin and E.A. Absolutely all three are masters at what they do. I have to say, I see and identify a piece of my personality in each mentor. As previously mentioned, Bill had done a demonic birth chart analysis for me. Bill and I discussed a lot about what occurred during the week and put the puzzle pieces together. We discussed the death ritual that E.A. did for me with Abaddon.

Everything each of my mentors brings up is not coincidence. It is in line with events, because in a previous reading Bill had said I was going through a period of death and rebirth. I knew this already. I had given up my old life, old friends, and severed many ties. My planetary healing was ALL about this as well, and the two people do not know each other. E.A. performed the ritual based on Abaddon, not by his choice.

After the ritual, Bill recommended I do a cut and clear and a removal of all past-life contracts and obligations that may no longer serve me as a continuation of that ritual E.A. performed. I am going to be completely honest. THIS LITTLE LHP GIRL WHO NEVER RESISTS? She resisted for a few minutes, and

I must tell you this secret: I ABSOFUCKINGLUTELY DID NOT WANT TO DO THIS. I told Bill it was definitely food for thought. My honesty and integrity will not let me lie and say sure and then not do it. Why did I not want to do it so adamantly in my soul? I had to really reflect on this. What was I holding on to and what was my fear? I immediately went to J, but I had only the day before given J the message I was letting him go freely with love and no longer communicating with him. So, was that really it? I knew J and I were finished. I had no idea what the fear was regarding cutting the ties.

***

I had a long conversation with my soul brother, as I like to call 777, of ClaviculaNoxBoutique. We discussed cutting ties, the grief of loss of J. I had just severed all ties to a client who had shredded my boundaries and destroyed a part of my personal life intentionally. No matter how much I tried to show this client how to find his worth and value, he threw it away, unwilling to do any work. There comes a point where you must stop and say no amount of money is worth your sanity, losing your own value, or your peace. That was that day, and it was a hard day for me because no healer, no magician, wants to feel like a loser who has had to give up on someone. I knew I was not giving up in my head. The businessperson knew I had made the right choice. The healer knew I had made the right choice for me and the client. However, me, the person, was not sitting well with it and I needed to sound off on this amazing and talented necromancer. His wise counsel is to always simply listen, never advise, as I do for him.

Giving advice to friends is the worst advice ever by the way. Never do it, my only advice. 777 actually said, "LuciaB, maybe you should consider it and clean up anything left from the past, any shamanic pacts, anything left over from J, anything that no longer serves you, and then take a few days of no work, just heal yourself. You are exhausted. Let the ritual absorb."

To hear his advice was so profound, I realized I was resisting because I was afraid of more loss. Not simply J but losing more than J. Losing J in this lifetime and giving him a gift of his happiness over mine and not fighting for us was the right choice, yet it was painful, and I needed time to really heal from that. But all the guys were right. I needed to do it and once my mind was made up it was time to do it now. Why now? A multitude of reasons. I did not want to back out and I needed to do this before the new moon in a few days.

***

One thing I have learned in this life is the preparation of the ritual is in part the biggest part of the ritual for me in a sense. I have four altars in my altar room, each facing in the elemental direction for a specific purpose with each Gatekeeper's direction in mind, and I adjust for the ritual at hand, adding anything apropos as needed, and I meditate prior to my ritual with what is appropriate.

With this ritual I did a self-healing meditation from the Monroe Institute I had recently downloaded in preparation, and I took a cleansing bath with Astarte and Juniper bath salts as I listened to a self-healing guided meditation. When I was finished, I went into my altar room and shut the door, breathing in the scents of all the wonderful aromas to be had of the heady perfumed incenses stored. I looked through my gems and crystals and chose the perfect offering for this ritual and placed it on my altar. I gathered my tools and thoughts as I lit the candles and summoned the entities required. I was no longer resistant to this ritual and was willingly falling into it and building the energy required to fulfill this task I previously denied myself of.

In this ritual Asmodeus and Lucifuge Rofocale as my co-patrons were most prevalent and spoke most. I prefer channeling over any form of ritual work. I write during rituals what I feel, sense, and see and I feel strongest in doing this form of work. Many magicians have a preference of work, and this I have found is mine.

It came to me that I had to cut ties to all previous healing contracts in past lives; that I had a soul tie to my mother that was extremely toxic and as long as that was carried into this life, I would resent it and her. We worked together in a past life as nurses in a military unit and I have been beholden to her ever since because she helped me save J from a severed arm in battle during WWII. That was a tie I gleefully cut and hacked at with a frenzy—sitting there shredding that with a chainsaw, grateful for the help given but ever so thankful it was over. I have given so much to this woman who hated me, and I never understood why I have given and given and gotten nothing in return. Even in her death I have gotten no answers when channeling a medium; not even my own gifts have given answers. I have peace now with this and I can completely let it go and know it is done.

It came to me as well that J and I have had a few past life contracts and in the last one we agreed to meet in this one and that our twin soulmate was eternal. I met with him eye to eye in energy and tearfully told him I released him and that I meant the text previously that a perfect love has no ties and no binds. I was letting him out of all previous agreements from past lives and even in the current life we had; unconditional love was unconditional and perfect and forgiving, and I released him from it. I told him with energy how much I loved him; I loved all the lessons and memories we have shared; the value he has given me was immeasurable, but it was his time to fly now. He had to heal and find his path and only he knew his happiness and where that path led; he could not find it with a leash tied to anyone and I was releasing him from all obligations. I sobbed after dismissing him because I felt this loss to my bone. This man has completed my soul. As I type these words I tear up because there is an emptiness where he should be. I rarely speak in anger; it is something you cannot take back. I can blame others for losing J. Games, magickal mischief, but it is down to me really: words I said in anger that cannot be undone. Irreparable harm adds up and damages people. It takes a toll on the people you love. He had repeatedly told me my words hurt him, and he had come back and tried to fix it; my fears, at that time, were huge with J, and I rebelled. Some things are just too great to fix. Could I do magick and undo it? Yes. But that would be cheating, and I would rather lose him fairly and allow him to work through his own things honestly than cheat him of learning his own lessons and know I had won unfairly. I had to learn a valuable lesson in this cut and clear. I hate words in anger yet I spoke them. I had to own my errors during this ritual in a harsh confronting of my part of the demise of the love of my life. It was not just magickal malice of others. I played a part. He played a part. Our past hurt and trauma played a part. We must be big enough people to fix it, and these are the consequences of actions that being a God in our own right plays. You must be mature enough to understand that sometimes you own your mistakes and apologies are not enough for the other person to get past. They are enough to move on and let go.

We all have pasts; we all have issues that crop up from our pasts and sometimes they shadow our present. You must decide in and of yourself what you are willing to let go of for love, for yourself, for the person you are genuinely in love with, to move on. I had to accept J had reached his limit and had nothing left for me.

The next point and layer revealed to me by my patrons were my mentors. I had no past life contract with them, but I had a fear of losing them. I had to address that fear. It boiled down to abandonment, which really pissed me off because that has been a thread in my life. Abandonment.

I cursed Abaddon because it felt to me that fall and fly issue that he told me about and the destruction of self (I know that may not make sense to some of you.) connected and resonated with me in that moment of time. I had to look at my mentors with a unique perspective. What was my fear? Of failing them? Of them failing me? There were a few issues from the week, with the LHP Convention, with the Gatekeepers' Challenge, that were all tied together, and I had to honestly dig deep and ask myself what was the issue? I questioned integrity, honesty, leadership, the path, myself, them. If I had no past contracts, why were they even being brought up?

It dawned on me. Service to others. I have had so many lives of service. I was a caretaker. I believe I have an xx caretaker gene and have even scheduled the test with radionics.us, which I have registered luciabelia.com with to boost my company certification. I needed to release service. Normally, with a mentor-mentee contract the mentee releases. My patrons wanted me to offer them the option to remove themselves as a way for me to fly by falling into the freefall abyss. I was releasing myself from all prior service contracts and fears of abandonment and by doing this with my current mentors, I was showing myself I had no fears now. I would not be abandoned, and I was not going to be abandoned because if any of them chose to leave I was going to be ok on my own. Lucifuge told me I was not going to like E.A.'s response. I was told it would rub me the wrong way and to lean into it. Embrace it. Love it because he was going to be honest. Respect it.

I was not happy with E.A.'s answer. It was honest. It was needed. I find a lot of people do not understand me. I find a lot of people can only read parts of me and that is something I need to accept. E.A. knows me a great deal and we connect extremely well, and he was not wrong to a great degree. But parts of what he said were not exactly right either. For the most part he said what was needed. I took on board what was needed and let go of what was not. I decided to investigate the parts I felt were not needed because if they were said, it is food for thought and can be digested and pondered. I do not confront to be confrontational, nor do I confront to be antagonistic. I am not a mean-spirited person, but

I will not back down either. I also chose my battles wisely. When a challenge is presented? It is accepted. E.A. challenges me and I like that. Not in a bad way, but to rise up and to be the best me I possibly can. He once compared my mentors to CCs from boot camp—each one having and taking on different personalities to push, provoke, and evoke emotions to get me to where I need to be. For the most part, I believe this. Unfortunately, mentors are human too; they have lives, and they make mistakes. And some mentors, as good and as academic as they are? They are not in it for the long haul, and they serve their purpose quickly. It is important to learn the lessons of who stays in your life and who fulfills their purpose quickly. When you learn this lesson? You have become a master.

When I finished my ritual, I was told to write to each mentor and offer to have them excuse themselves, which I did. I was also challenged to give this offer to a few close friends. I was a little confused but did not resist. What was the point, purpose, and reason behind all things Gatekeepers being equal, right? I knew Asmodeus had a reason for doing it, and I was annoyed but knew he was flushing something beyond my knowledge out and it would have purpose, so I did it.

***

I decided after the ritual that I needed a healing done. I felt out of sorts, and I had a lot of work to do. I decided to confront a fear of the Wire Bridge. The Wire Bridge was a place special to J and I. We started going in July. He had seen the lights were broken and he told me since it was our special place, he was going to fix the lights. He actually restrung the lights on

Thanksgiving Day, he and ten men. It was a monumental job and work of love for me.

I went after avoiding it for months. I brought a crystal for Hecate and drew her sigil in the snowy banks of the river and meditated. As I walked the bridge, reliving beautiful memories of my lover and I there, I released all my anger at my loss. I read the love stories of people written on the metal and on the wooden shingles and I released my anger at the destruction caused in my life. I lifted J up because he showed love not by destruction but by forever giving by stringing lights. I texted my gratitude to him by explaining this thought to him. I went down to the snowy base of the bridge and gave Hecate her cross crystal and thanked her for listening to me and healing me. I placed the crystal deep into the base of the bridge forming a five-way cross inside the base of the bridge's rock formation and chanted her Enn for a little while finding peace. I fought the tears, refusing to let them fall—instead, manifesting them as energy and pointed that as healing towards J, for his happiness, and his success as his busy season is about to start. I pointed it towards his home life, wanting him to know how much he has meant to me. Knowing the anger was completely gone as was the sadness, I had come to terms with the loss of J. I was looking forward to my life, even knowing it was going to be solitary. It was a choice I was ok with. When you find someone who completes you in every way, no one else works. I knew I was not going to look and would just throw myself into my business and be good with that.

I was given friendships with people who genuinely cared for and about me and that was new. They did not replace J, but it was better than nothing and I was fine alone. I preferred a solitary life more than a social one. So many people misjudged me, thinking of me as a social butterfly based on my looks, how I have lived, how I dress, or how I speak. I am tiny, at 5'4" and 110 pounds, and I am constantly underestimated. I was always told I did not belong here by J. But I am here, I am happy in the woods of Maine, and I am thriving. I learn as I go. You can pick me up and drop me anywhere in the world and I will survive because I have no choice. In the end? Everyone leaves and I am on my own and I have always survived.

***

When I arrived home from the Wire Bridge, I was met with uproar to my 100-acre paradise. The caretaker was driving the roads like a madman hunting, and the kids next door were stuck on the side of the house and told not to wander. Curious as to the happenings, I asked my neighbor and was told I had had a visitor in the early hours close to sunrise. I did not realize it because I was so busy sending out my missives to the people in my lives giving them permission to leave me and cutting soul ties from my past lives that I missed the mountain cougar less than three feet from my front door pacing back and forth. I went out and took photos of her big paw prints two feet from my front steps and sent them to a few friends and to J, who lives nearby on 100 acres himself. It is a rare thing to get a mountain cougar this close to a home in Maine. They are everywhere, but they do not normally venture this close to homes, unlike the squirrels, and raccoons, et al. They are not tame. As spring is coming, she may have been hungry and wanted to feed, but my heart knew the visit was spiritual. She was there for me. She was three feet away from me on the living room couch watching and she was three feet away from my trash bins, and she had made no attempt to get into them to forage. The saying when you get a visit from a mountain cougar is protection, motherhood, renewal, reuniting. I knew in that moment as I got the alert from messenger that J had texted that things were opening again between us. The cougar was telling me to not give up and she would protect me. I had to do the Hecate Ritual. The cougar was Mother Hecate at work. Ever-present, ever-loving. When you do your shadow work and release what is right, what is not for you leaves, but what is meant stays. J stayed. He is fighting for us in ways he can and struggling in his own ways; I realized he and I are a work in progress. We have a long road back to recovery and recovery may be just friends. The road is long, narrow, wide, twisting and we both have a say in this path, so only time will tell where we will end up. Healing is a three-way street—his, mine, and ours.

***

As part of my Gatekeepers' Challenge and tribute to the Gatekeepers I was told to do a guided meditation in honor of each one. I did it and was able to find a great sound engineer named Dane Howard. He created amazing, dark ambient music for me that I have the rights to, and I created a special meditation for each gatekeeper. I offered this to E.A. because he is the Gatekeepers, in essence. I told him during my boot camp with him that he should really trademark this. I am not sure why. It is not an enforceable issue; it is more that this is his creation. I have been told by several Gatekeepers: I am in them; they are in me. But I have been told by all the Gatekeepers, E.A. is the tenth Gatekeeper. They have, during my months of training, hinted he needed to write and create the tenth Gatekeeper, they have told me to prod him and provoke and tease him throughout our sessions without giving me full details, but it did come out with sweet Lucifuge Rofocale that E.A. is the tenth, not just the keeper of the keys, but the tenth. I created the nine and they are as follows. I believe it needs to be a set of ten with E.A. and his storm meditation as the complete set:

1. Lucifuge: a journey of healing into the underworld

2. Healing into the black flame with Azazel

3. Healing with Belial the lawless

4. Finding your balance with Lord Asmodeus

5. Connecting and creating with Lord Ba'al

6. Deep within the Abyss with Lord Abaddon

7. Lord Lucifer, the Enlightened One

8. Questioning with Lord Beelzebub

9. Finding your purpose with Satan

I found that much of what I was able to do with the meditations came from discussions with E.A., and a few terms came from his books. A lot came from my time with the Gatekeepers but, in general, the Gatekeepers to me is E.A. and his work, so it must be shared. Doing the right thing is important to me and it doesn't matter what E.A. decides, you have to make choices in life that serve your conscience and you have to do what is right for you in the long run. You cannot do it for appearances, or to make friends. You must do what you can live with. People are going to think what they think about you whether you put your jeans on the left leg or the right leg first, so at the end of the day do what best serves you. Be a leader and let others follow you. Set an example of what you want done to you and if people do not accept, or do not comprehend your behavior, then let them learn. I am not saying E.A. did not understand because he did; I am saying in general. So many people are out for themselves, or see a good deed wrapped in a riddle of self-service, greed, strings attached, and angles. I believe we, as LHP, need to start making progress towards setting and resetting boundaries and standards into making us a better community. We need to be better stewards of our own kingdom and better stewards to others.

People can laugh and say, "Wow, rich coming from a convicted felon," but if you do not know me, do not judge me, because I do not judge you. We are all filled with a primal grace, a dignity that is deep within, and no one has the right to extinguish our black flame. I have worked extremely hard to grow, to change, and to remove a stigma put on me that was not true, much less the stigma I put on myself.

We, as a community, must learn and grow to protect each other against the outside because it is coming. Shadow work is extremely difficult, and I have come a long way. Gatekeeper work is extremely difficult and let me tell you, I did the fucking work. The journey since November was hard. I persevered. I did twenty-hour days to get the task done that Satan set before me.

They kept changing the end zone and I accepted it graciously because I understood. I was told many things with my gifts, and I realized they knew things were going to change. They only told me what they knew my human brain could cope with. It is why they gave me mentors; it is why they gave me stages. It is why they gave me two patrons. They gave me a heavy load to carry, and I have done it. My parroting of "what is my next step?" grew old, but it is familiar to me now and comforting. When I went to boot camp? I was ready for anything and everything coming my way because I knew a shitstorm was coming.

Chapter 13

The Test of the Rubber Hitting the Road: Boot Camp

Where to start with boot camp? Prior to leaving for my boot camp there was a shitstorm hitting on every front. The client I had removed came to me and begged for a chance. Things were brought to light, and we did a destruction ritual. I saw parts of my past were mingled in with his and I allowed the chance. When people are sincere and honest, I always give them a chance.

We did several healings. I stood firm; no life coaching but would do the rituals. When I got back from boot camp and after talking to E.A., we would see what he and I felt about doing any further work. E.A. had done work with him, and he felt the same as I that this was someone who did not appreciate work being done and threw away any energy or work being done for him. I call them "energy vampires," and the "what is next?" curse. This client drained me emotionally and physically. I did see psychically that the changes, the healing, and destruction of the patterns he displayed had helped, but I wanted time to see what was what before I committed to anything else.

***

On the Friday I was to leave for Boston for my flight out west, I was offered a travel-safe ritual, from "a friend and colleague." I accepted and paid for it because I do not like to take advantage. I had a great three-hour ride to Boston. I stopped to get my mani-pedi along the way and stopped in New Hampshire to do a few messages; I was in no hurry. I had all day to enjoy the sun and warm weather. J and I were texting like little kids. I enjoyed the hotel and room service salad. Sure. Sounds great, right?

I felt blessed my friend had thought of me for this ritual, especially since in the past she had issues with E.A., and I had had to constantly correct her bad behavior regarding him that I found offensive. She had never met him, but I had always felt a "jilted lover" vibe. When I had previously confronted her, she denied it—simply stating his past legal issues, etc. However, his legal issues are not hers, and the press overdramatizes things. I know from personal experience, as should she since her brother is serving a major sentence and no one throws it in her face. Most of E.A. and his publicity is not his own doing but reporters gossiping about things outside of his control or freaks and geeks wanting to be E.A. Koetting.

Oddly enough, my smooth ride ended shortly around 11:00 p.m. I had gotten off the phone with my dearest brother friend 777 of ClaviculaNoxBoutique. I ended up spending the night, not on my beautifully appointed bed at the Hyatt Harbourshores, but on the marble-floored bathroom retching and convulsing after eating a salad and a cappuccino. Yes, an arugula salad with peaches and goat cheese fell me that night. I was texting J profound messages about us that I received while writhing on the floor because it hit me. I did not give anyone my flight plans, or itinerary; I was living a solitary life. He had called me the day before, giddy with love and admiration from a hand-carved box I had sent to him with a hand-carved postcard of a photo of his destroyed plane, and the message, "All good pilots find their way home in any storm." I had done this because he had told me he felt he was circling the drain. I was concerned and I wanted him to know regardless of where we were at in our relationship or non-relationship, I was always, always right there with unconditional love supporting him. Even if he was unable to return it right now because we were beyond soulmates, we were each other inside out. A year ago, he had written an email telling me we walked in each other's footsteps a decade apart and he was right, telling me it took Putin's war to have us reunite. J is a prolific writer himself if he only trusted his gifts—very profound and gifted psychically as well.

***

I woke up and made my 8:00 a.m. flight to Charlotte. It was not the best flight due to storms. We arrived and were stuck on the tarmac for over an hour. When I got to my connecting flight, they had just locked the gate. I struggled to get a new flight. Extremely frustrated, my Vegas flight appeared to be THE ONLY ON TIME FLIGHT THAT DAY!!

As I sat in the Admirals Club planning the next steps, I was frustrated because my plan to get to Vegas and relax before all hell broke loose was not going to happen. I was not due to arrive now until 7:15 p.m. I had a 10:30 p.m. meditation with Courtney Worhling, and a midnight six-hour workshop with the Monroe Institute, which is why I had flown out a day early. I was still not 100% from the night before and my radar and ESP was not ok due to the "ritual" done for me. Normally, I am the best traveler, and nothing ever goes wrong for me. Ever.

My Spidey senses were sensing criminal mischief and mayhem, so to speak, and I was fuming. WTF. All you can do in this time of drama is breathe and refuse to be drawn into the fray. I breathed. I told Hecate I was not being challenged today. I enjoyed the Admirals Club, and relaxed. When I got to Vegas eventually, my luggage was not there. Huh. Lol.

Well, what can you do right? You can get mad and scream and go off on attendants or you can ask them what they suggest. I was told to come back in ninety minutes when my luggage arrived, or they could bring it to my hotel in four to six hours. Ahhhh, I will be back. No brainer, get my rental car and come back. After all the messages were done, my luggage arrived, and I was back at my hotel at 9:45 p.m. Thankfully, Courtney had to cancel for personal reasons. I was kindly upgraded at the Palazzo to a suite and ordered room service. I decided it was bed and not the meditation course for me and sent a message to Leidi in the Netherlands. Little did I know that poor 777 was not included in his own link and was needing me to get him access to the class I talked him into taking. Hahahaha. He is such a great guy; he shrugged it off when he realized what had happened. We will do the class in June together. That is a real friend and brother in the LHP who does not get mad that I bailed and did not get mad that he missed his course. He found the login, but he was refused entry because he was a few minutes late and she did not want to "disrupt the rest of the group."

Some people take things too seriously. In addition, she should have tailored the six-hour class to the people in the class; everyone except her and two Europeans were in North America. It was not right the class was at midnight (or 3:00 a.m. even for some) and noonish for her. Everyone in North America fell asleep and missed most of the training. I want to get trained in how to facilitate this and take over because we are lacking in how we treat clients if we cater to the facilitators' needs, not the clients', who are paying for the service. 3:00 a.m. is a tough time to do a class on meditation. Start at a time that serves the greater good of all involved, just my humble opinion.

Meditation is serious work, I completely understand, but when you do not send a student a link and they do the work to get to the class, even five or ten minutes late, that is on you. Let them in, they obviously want to learn.

I woke up the next day refreshed and ready to conquer the world. Ok, not the world, but at least Vegas. I got a welcome text from E.A. I decided to relax and get a massage and a hair blowout before my eye exam. I could not get this done back home, being the responsible Satan's emissary and all.

All things relative, the massage was amazing, and the blowout was superb. My hair is thick, long, and extremely curly. It is mid-back and I do not like to shampoo, tame it, comb it, much less blow-dry it, so I love to get it done. I love the time with the hairdresser catching up on what is going on in their lives, because it is not my work. I do not have to do anything but sit and laugh. I enjoy that time. It is decadent for most, but it is my self-care, and as a Leo? We care for our hair; it is vanity to most, but essential to us. Our mane is our main attraction, they say, lol. My long locks are a labor of love and I have no problem turning them over to someone else occasionally.

My eye exam. Well, let me say this. For years, I have struggled. I use multifocal dailies and I still must use readers because for whatever reason the eye doctor I go to cannot get it right. This one in Lenscrafters in Las Vegas Fashion Mall? Dr. Mitchell Nash? WHAT A TREAT! He is old-school, and I cannot say enough for old-school. His first comment was, "Let me start out by saying I do this the old way." I was in love. We did it the old way—do not get me wrong, we did all the fancy machines, pictures, puffs, scopes—but he broke it down old-school. I was diagnosed with a small astigmatism. I was diagnosed properly, and he explained why I was still needing readers. He explained why I have trouble seeing red when every other optician has laughed at me when I tell them I have trouble seeing colors. He was retired as the NASA optician before coming to Vegas to work, and I tell you this, I felt pampered, and I would have given a kidney to get that eye exam. My eyes are grey-blue, super sensitive to any light, and in the last two years, I have lost quite a lot of vision going from 20/20 to what I have now. I was fitted with the right prescription for my multifocal, and I was given a great fit for glasses that are, as we speak, getting shipped to me here at home. I was told to stay away from red dashboards as my vision issue cannot pick up red spectrums because it is too far on the distance of the rainbow and to stick with blue and greens. Good to know because I really struggle with any hue of red and if you ask me shades, I cannot tell them apart.

I laughed during a ritual with Eric because I had done my pact in Dragon's Blood ink, and I could barely read it. I mean contacts, glasses, and shifting the paper in and around the light tilting kind of reading. We both laughed, but I had written it without even thinking about it. I am going to have to drop food coloring into my inks so I can pick it up in future rituals because the color hurts my eyes.

***

I arrived in Hurricane Utah that night and checked in prior to boot camp ready, rested, and prepared for what lay ahead. We had decided to meet up at a local café for breakfast and when we met I had to hug him because he is a huggable guy. E.A. has a profound way of knowing and saying things ahead of time that he may not yet know are profound. On the Thursday before I had left, he had asked me about a specific person, and it had no real relevance at the time because it had not happened. I was bubbling over to share the journey story and the belief I had been cursed and not highly favored as believed. We both looked at each other and knew it to be true because of previous conversations. We both felt this person did not realize they had done it, but felt it was important when we got to the temple to investigate it and ascertain what was next.

Talking to E.A. over breakfast was like a psychic surgical dump. He felt like a shrink, a brother, a friend, and a mentor all-in-one. I could not wait to get started on our journey of magickal mayhem. We set up our schedule of what was next: discussing my pact with Lucifuge, the issues with J and the healing, the labyrinth we were going to walk and a destruction ritual with

Choronzon I was going to perform. We had a lot to do in a little time and I was so excited.

I had a lot of anger under the surface because one of the things we touched on was the LHP and the consortium collapsing. I was annoyed in general about how the presenters were treated. I am annoyed at how it went down in general, and how the attendees were treated because I still have not been officially told the people I was paying to see are not attending. Poor leadership. It is why Satan was pushing me on the trajectory I was on. I had known since November it was going to implode. We touched base on this, and we discussed the caretaker vial I had been sent and how the download spoke to me being a xx-caretaker healer/protector and what that means for me moving forward. I felt annoyance at the person who sent it to me with no instruction, who is not a caretaker himself, and the lack of information, in general. I had, at first, not felt anything other than annoyance at the lack of information disseminated with the package. I had told him to cancel the order before he sent it, but he canceled my membership instead and sent the caretaker. Once I got over the irritation and focused on the download, I realized it did, in fact, speak to me. The guy then tried to belittle me, saying I was obviously not a caretaker, and it was ok, to send the vial back; it was not for everyone. I believe it was because I had admonished him for how he handled it, that he sent a tube with nothing and no instruction, no note, and it was irresponsible to the caretakers out there how to find one another.

Oh, well. I heard my message and I decided to follow my guides and gather the LHP caretakers ourselves. E.A. and I put the vial on his radionics machine, and we shot it out there and sent it to whom we felt needed it. E.A. got his message and he can share it himself; another person I felt needed it came back receiving his download. I believe the next will receive the tube shortly with what I have discerned his message is for him moving forward. I do not beat to anyone else's drum; I do not believe it is right simply because they say so. Especially when they cannot give answers. I follow the path I am told. My patrons have shown me the way and when both E.A. and I get similar messages? Who am I to argue?

***

The first thing we did arriving at his amazing temple space was sit at his crystal and scry regarding the curse sent to me. We both saw and felt the same image: a skull with a knife. Ahhh, yeah. Thanks, friend. Love you too. We immediately did a binding and returned it to sender. Little did we know . . .

We moved on and started doing my pact. I am going to tell you that I love to write pacts. I get great joy out of writing pacts. This pact with Lucifuge Rofocale that Right Reverend Bill Duvendack had done a ritual for, that I was told to do an actual pact for, was no exception. I was, for whatever reason, led to leave the first page's backside blank, something I NORMALLY never do. It was two pages of sheep parchment full.

I presented it to Lucifuge Rofocale, but before we even started the ritual Azazel showed up, and then all the Gatekeepers were there. I knew this was NOT going to be an ordinary pact ritual. E.A. and I looked at each other, smirked, and shook our heads. All nine wanted in on this deal and a paragraph was inserted on all nine's behalves. I have never heard of this before, but it is not the first time they have done this to me.

I had previously given homage to Lucifuge and was going to get a tattoo on my ankle for him and they all insisted on a tattoo. I ended up having to get it on my foot, and they then insisted I get my sigil on the center of all of them. It was funny at the time; in hindsight, not funny trying to fit ten sigils on a size five foot, and not look lopsided. I refused the color tattoo because I do not get color tattoos. I did win that war but at the end of the day it was exhausting going in for one and coming out with ten. It was like the day I was possessed by all nine at once. Chaos, calamity, and no leader whatsoever, a pig pile in and a bruising of my body, except with the tattoo I did not bruise nor bleed nor flake, I merrily had a swollen foot from the tattoos themselves.

***

After the pact was finished and I passed it around the triangle of candles and incense, I looked to see if it was signed by Lucifuge. E.A. and I looked at it at the same time, then at each other, and our jaws hit the floor. It was not signed in the typical place, and it was not signed by merrily Lucifuge. It had twenty-seven symbols throughout the pact: obvious symbols, sigils, and demonic symbology in the spaces between my words, in the columns and everywhere in between. The craziest part was they were in sets of three and five single symbols. Three were tridents. Just that morning, 777 of ClaviculaNoxBoutique had just texted me the photo of Azazel's trident sigil to see what I thought of it, because he felt it relevant to me. Two of the tridents were Azazel, we realized. We confirmed one trident belonged to Lucifer from the Grimoire of the Verium. 777 has identified over eight of the sigils and symbols because he is an expert at such things, and he hates to be stumped. Needless to say, the Gatekeepers approved my pact. I went over the symbols and sigils with E.A.'s help with a highlighter to not lose these amazing gifts from the Gatekeepers. I am attaching them for all to see because I believe it is a gift to share. I firmly believe the LHP in general needs to become more concentric as a community and pull together and share information better—to pull resources, to pull together in crisis instead of apart and pointing fingers. We get enough of that from the outside. We do not need to implode from within.

E.A. and I discussed J: how I was feeling, our communication, that we were not letting go of each other, and that I was frustrated he was still in his situation and that he had told me he was circling the drain. We decided to print a few pictures and perform a few healing rituals for him. I think those were the two hardest rituals I have ever performed, honestly, because I personally do not like performing rituals on myself or people close to me. I feel explosive. I feel chaotic inside when I do them. I know it was the right thing to do and avoiding doing these is a disservice because my connection is the strength, the power, the harness of healing in a sense that can make the difference, but it also drains me. It has a way of killing a part of me for a long period after and it is something I need to work on internally. During the ritual I was taken on a journey with J of his path and history. I held him during the trauma, telling him he was not alone, and several times I took the beatings and pain for him. It was a significant journey for me because I needed to see what was holding him back, what was stopping him from crossing the line from point A to point B. The ritual continued with a photo of him and I at our bridge. I teared up when during the ritual his throat chakra burned, revealing he felt he had no voice. E.A. and I did our best to heal this for him. I needed to sit with this for a time to meditate on if I was to blame in part—if me pushing him to remember our love was restricting the imbalance. I was truly not comfortable causing this gentle soul pain. I ended the ritual putting the photos back-to-back to represent that I would always have his back always and forever, in spirit and in energy, as a friend, as a healer, and as a role of protector. So mote it be, as it shall be, so shall it be. I felt the healing take place and I sent it forwards to J. I realized in the past I kept trying to walk away, give up, cut ties because I was afraid of loss, but in doing so, I was living fear-based, and I could not give up on us. It was like losing a limb, a part of me, by giving up on us. When I walk away from J, I feel lost; breathless; not heartbroken, simply, a feeling of emptiness; a part of me is missing, misplaced; I get tired easily, like when my iron is low, or my blood is not oxygenated. I am not depressed; things feel like they are coming to me through a funnel. I do not like that feeling and if I must fight for what I know to be right, I will for the time being fight fair.

J oddly enough sent me a text shortly after the ritual answering a text that I had sent days ago. I had to laugh. The universe is good. Games are certainly afoot. J was not happy I was with E.A. but J being J cannot find the words and cannot say, "I do not like you being away from home." So instead, he says he was out of town as well when I asked him to pick up a generator. I had responded days earlier why and where. It took us doing the ritual to get a single response, sulkily, "working." SMH, it was a response and I took it gladly because J was not pleased I was working out of town. Whether he sees it or not, and whether we are together or not, he gets possessive of me, of my time, and he was still stinging from our telephone call the other day when I had to end it shortly to finish an appointment. J does not like me telling him what we are going to do with each other, and I have been deciding we are not working because of M and her constant interference. He wants us to get along, he wants things to work out in their own time and he wants patience. I am tired of patience, and I am tired of being put off. Butting heads is exhausting and patience is thin; there is a fine line to the dance in life between love and war.

Another ritual E.A. and I performed during my time with him was amazing, and it was with Choronzon. Many people are afraid to approach Choronzon, but I found the destructive powers of Choronzon to be healing. I put all the pain, the anger, the rage of my stalker and his behavior over the last six years, into this ritual. It was an amazing and powerful release, and I did not have any blowback from using Choronzon, the master of dispersion and hallucination and yes, yet again all the Gatekeepers were present and accounted for. Oddly, the one thing that did come out during this ritual was when E.A. summoned Amaymon he said with great humor, "No, nope, not me, I am not with you today." E.A. was so surprised that he had to start the ritual over and we all laughed at this.

During our evocations and working to date during my time
with E.A., Lucifuge had come up behind us, which is how he
typically does with me, and on a previous evocation I had said,
"For the love of fuck, why can't you approach from the front,
ever?"

So, in this ritual when he was summoning Lucifuge, he
again stopped and looked at me strangely on my throne he had
given me to sit upon. He laughed, saying, "Hey, Lucia, where do
you want Lucifuge?"

I cheekily said, "Right here in front of me."

My co-patron kindly obliged and after the ritual we had
a great laugh at that one because I was given the choice. We
tried to figure out why the Gatekeepers were not wanting me
to work with Amaymon yet, and I believed at the time it had
to do with the riddle I had solved with Lord Lucifer, but all was
to be revealed when I arrived home by my two Patrons, Lord
Asmodeus and Lord Lucifuge posthaste.

The walk in the labyrinth with E.A. was great fun. It was
healing and revealed a lot as well. As I had said, I was led to him.
We are both parts of a storm necessary to work, but equal and
reactive. There is another component to the storm. I realized
during the labyrinth journey that there were three mountains
and three separate phases of storm clouds above us, and I had
told E.A. and shown him the phases. As we were about to leave,
what I had said materialized, and the secret is ours to carry, and
no, neither storm nor rain appeared. All will be revealed in the
end. It was a beautiful journey with my mentor and Lord Azazel,
who was the one to send me to the desert in the first place, was

laughing at us as we walked the Labyrinth saying things like "When I sent you to the desert, Lucia, I was not exactly expecting you to walk between rocks, but if you must why are you walking the straight and narrow and not stepping over the rocks onto the next step? I am surprised you are both staying within the lines to the center, each on your own journey, but getting there together in the end, as all nine of us have ACTUALLY SAID!" It is funny because I do not resist and knew all along the process would lead me to the center. I knew I would eventually work with E.A., to some degree. He, because of his past journey with people, has often said, "Satan and the Gatekeepers do not choose, I choose." Ahhh, very true E.A. But sometimes the universe chooses for us.

I realized that since November the Gatekeepers have been preparing me to become a master because there is a major split happening in the Left Hand Path. They knew that the consortium was not going to happen, because they were not going to let it happen. They wanted me ready for when it fractured to be in a position to be their queen on the chessboard. I am, not to brag, an amazing strategist. I see four steps ahead without my gift. I am already playing Chess when everyone is playing Checkers and I play for keeps. I am competitive within myself while others are busy competing amongst themselves. They do not learn that competing against others is a waste of time; we are all unique, we are all individuals, and we do not compare. Sadly, when you do not figure that out, you destroy yourself.

I have learned through this journey into the Left Hand Path; through the path work with the Gatekeepers; working with E.A., Martin McGreggor, Right Reverend Bill Duvendack; a month with Mammon; creating rituals like the Mulcifer "Architect," a highly sophisticated creative ritual; the Prometheus work; "Stealing Fire from the Gods" ritual and working with Choronzon; learning the Grigori; working with the Dark Goddesses; not to mention getting my iNLP in life coaching, advanced hypnotherapy, having E.A. teach me the basics of Radionics, and taking Blackwitchcoven's demonic course, that life is going to hit you whether you want it to or not. You must come together as a spiritual system, or you will fail.

That is what this Gatekeepers' Challenge Satan tossed at my feet was all about. He has known me since I was a little girl. He has been there for me during every crisis of my life. I have survived death three times because of the Gatekeepers. From a five-year-old overdosing on 500 Tylenol, a fifteen-foot slide fall, to a forty-year-old dying from MRSA and spending twelve weeks in an ICU getting unction—I hallucinated on morphine of him sledding on the infected white blood cells flowing through my body, moving forward to the overdose of the 50 Flexeril with him and Azazel in my hotel room forcing me to breathe for three days until I was found. I believe I survived many beatings as a kid and the burn of my face without major scars because of the work of Azazel.

I realized during my time with E.A. that I am extremely gifted in magick. I know, I sound egotistical, but you cannot do great magic without ego. I am saying this not to be coming from ego but to prove a point. I am a healer—a healer first and foremost. I received the caretaker tube download and it spoke to me telling me I was a protector of all tribes. That is the table I am going to sit at and head. Many people think healers are less than, little Fru white-magic entities who get a specific job done and are not capable of greatness or are not capable of being a master demonic magician at the same time. I have news for you. There are changes coming into this world. Momentous changes. The Gatekeepers are no longer happy with armchair magicians spouting off in their names in visions and conversations. There are doers and there are sayers. There are those who are good and those who are evil. Those two terms get interchanged depending on the context because those who do evil in the Gatekeepers' names are actually doing good, so do not get confused by the Judeo-Christian terms of good versus evil and think you are safe in the coming days, months, years. It is time to hone your skills. It is time to get out of your chairs and off your forums. Stop posting that you are doing the work; do the work and then post about it. I am not saying end time; I am saying changing time.

I have been given a vision and I am going to fulfill it because I called the LHP Consortium imploding in November 2022. I know my path. I became a Demonic Master Magician capable of greatness by the date the Gatekeepers set for me. I did what I set out to do. Phase I is completed. Phase II has started, and may the battle begin, because I am taking no prisoners. I have a dozen eggs. Two are bare. I am going to call this the Dragon's Egg of the Trapezoid because of previous meditations with the Gatekeepers and until I am told to call it otherwise, that is what it is for reasons I am not ready to disclose. I am Satan's emissary; I am his Adversary and when he told me I was his Eastern Star and he called me to rise? I did what was asked. I rose, I struggled,

I fell, and I picked myself back up and did it again every time. Many times heartbroken over the loss of J, often obsessed with thoughts of how I can fix us, yet always driven, always focused on what was expected of me, my ADHD always allowing me to multitask like an SOB. There are nine tables in the Dragon's Egg of the Trapezoid. Each person will head a table. They will know who they are when they receive the tube and the resin disc with the invitation to stand up and protect and serve what I no longer wish to call the Left Hand Path after what happened to the Consortium. Instead I will refer to it as the Path. Or DET.

We, as leaders, need to step up and carry forward our belief systems, stop being afraid of being exposed, stop being afraid of being sued, stop being afraid of being harassed, and stand together. United we stand, divided we fall created this Country. When one of us is attacked, when our belief system is attacked, we are all attacked. No more creating conventions, or gatherings in dark places. We have rights. When certain people with nothing better to do want to attack and cast ignorant falsehoods on our characters? Cease and desist letters need to be issued. We are not doing anything wrong. I personally am tired of being labeled. I did my sentence on a crime I felt I did not do. I am a felon, and it is something I must carry forever. It does not mean the person who put me in a prison gets to keep me in a prison, nor does it mean anyone else gets to keep me in a box because of my past. We all grow up. We all get to change, to do our shadow work, and to manifest into better people because that is what our path work, our entire spiritual system, is based on. And if you are practicing your actual belief of anything demonic, anything Godhood? You are a different person than you were yesterday because your ascension DEMANDS it. The Gatekeepers demand it, and you, as the King or Queen of your Infernal Empire, the keepers of your black flame within better be demanding it.

The first thing I do as a Demonic Master and healer every day is pull a tarot and ask what is my path today, what do I need to focus on? I then do a meditation and have my coffee. I am not perfect. I fuck up on a daily. Trust and believe I do. But I am perfect for me. I try. I do my work. I am consistent with the work I do, and I am actually doing the work I charge for. Integrity costs everything because it is priceless.

My word means everything to me, and when it was taken from me, I overdosed. I will never allow anyone to take my voice or my word again, and the next time someone tries to challenge my integrity? Good luck. I am not the same as I was several years ago. I am not afraid of the shadow anymore and I will come out swinging now. Back then I was suffering a lot of losses and did not really care what happened to me, and the person was doing me a favor. This time? I like myself. A lot. I value myself, my time, and my energy. Anyone who wants to fuck with me is going to learn a valuable lesson. I do not bother people, I do not judge people, and I do not bring war to people, so be warned, come to my Demonic Magick Healing Infernal Kingdom Empire in peace, or you will get a bloodbath. My co-patrons are not Lord Lucifuge Rofocale and Lord Asmodeus for nothing, and Lord Lucifuge Rofocale is now determined to make me an expert in the Dark Arts and as he says "Buttercup, you did so well, so fast, with the Gatekeepers' Challenge; you will be ready by the Samhain Event, nooooo problem."

***

I am going to look at J's actions moving forward. He has been amazingly supportive of me becoming a satanist, a demonic magician and healer, of me writing this book, and of me including him in this book. He has been patient and kind during the turmoil the last few months. He has never blocked me, even when I told him to. We have both been angry with each other over events since November, neither has fully walked away. I do not like loose strings; I find them cumbersome, and they always seem to come back and bite you later. I tend to worry about the string; J likes the string to dangle. I think he has won this battle of wills. I am not sure he will ever understand the loss because he ignores what he cannot have and works through it until bedtime and starts a new day fresh and rinses and repeats. I do not think he really regrets us, or our loss. I do not think he is worried about losing me or wanting us to work, and I think it is the healthy thing to do to let go and stop fighting the most stubborn man I know because, unfortunately? When I say he is me inside out, I am not joking. We are so identical, and I realize one of us is going to have to cave in this situation, and it is never ever going to be J showing up at my door or texting me an "I love you," or "Can we fix the holes in our boat today, LuciaBelia?"

I hate to end this book without a happily ever after, but life isn't perfect. Love is imperfect and sometimes someone loves someone, and it simply is not returned. You must be a grown-up about it, let it go, and love them regardless because you love them for reasons—not because they are good or bad people— but because they touch your soul, they make you laugh, or make you feel safe. With J, it was all the above. I am going to have to let him move on to his next journey with M, with whoever the next lover in his life is, knowing I was replaced, being ok with it, and accepting the pain that comes with it and breathing through it and growing. E.A. says to use that pain and channel great magick. That is what I am going to do.

Chapter 14
The Finale

In the end, I am always right regardless of if I am wrong because I survive, live, grow, and prosper. Every choice I make takes me on the path I was meant to be on, and I flourish. I do not manifest as the average person. I am not a victim; I am surrounded by means. It is me and I am it. It comes to me like a magnet by choice and situation and I am content. That is my life. I do not worry about money, situations, or events because I know it is fine.

My life lesson is to ask for "massive"? According to Abaddon, he wants me to learn to ask for much, much more. The Gatekeepers think I ask for too little so when I did my Lucifuge pact, I asked for the moon. In fact, I did not ask, I demanded and commanded because I am a God and I deserve it. I willed it into being. We as Satanists are a turbulent tribe, my mentor, Martin McGreggor, recently told me. We are not pacifists. We do not go peacefully into the day or night praying to a God for peace. We use demons, we shout into the night sky for liberation, we shake the trees, we rattle cages within our souls—we demand and command change within. We must lean into the storm that rages within us and find shelter and peace within the changes we create or crash on the rocks of life. I found great comfort with that. I looked at that statement intently as a healer: do I want a life in a pasture of a field grazing like a sheep, or do I want to seize it and grab hold for dear life and command my destiny each and every bumpy moment knowing it is taking me higher and higher on my ascent? We each must look inside ourselves and find that answer and when it comes? Buckle up and enjoy the ride. Otherwise, we may as well be sheep.

I am a healer. I am a protector, I am the winds of change and transformation, I am Left Hand Path, and I am a God. I will take the bumpy, rough road any day.

Doing the work you are supposed to do is hard. Doing it with integrity is even harder. You are supposed to have a path and a purpose in life and having Magick as an extension of yourself is not an easy life to lead. You want to have an easy fix in life and Magick is not an easy fix. It opens doors, it allows for healing, it provides purpose, it is a path. It does not give guarantees in life. That is the fine print of Satanism many forget to read when they think it is glamorous to say they are Satanist because it is fashionable or trendy to be a Satanist. It is hard to follow any Spiritual Path and to be true to yourself. It is even harder when you have opposition from the outside, and from within.

The reality is you have to be true to yourself because Magick, Satanism, Spirituality comes from within. It is genuinely an extension of yourself. Love has to be a part of that and self-love has to be the foundation of any Spiritual Belief you choose to follow. This was the key element that the Gatekeepers taught me that I had to bring forth into my healing practice.

Healing work is about using self-love and transferring it magickally to others as a tool. It is a form of self-sacrifice, dedication and craft honed through time, honoring traditions, skill and a real labor of love that you give to the Universe through Energy, that is constantly in motion. We, as healers must do this with a detached elegance and promote healing through Magickal Systems with grace and dignity regardless of what happens in our daily life, and for me, that was the greatest lesson that I learned, from E.A. Koetting, from the Gatekeepers, from all the realms I work with and moving forward with J. I learned to detach with love.

I, most importantly, while working with Santa Muerte, learned to bring into my healing practice that life is not a race, learning skills is not a race, and that stepping back and turning into yourself is an art form. I rose to Satan's Challenge because time was of the essence, and I am glad I did it. But I was not arrogant enough to believe I was supposed to stop there, that I was the best version of myself, or better than anyone else. I had merely accomplished a challenge of where I needed to be at a specific time, for a specific goal with a specific Mastery of the Dark Arts. You are never perfect, you never know enough, and you must forge ahead.

I recently received a correspondence from E.A. suggesting I may not need his assistance as I possibly had surpassed his skills. I laughed because I knew he was teasing me. I will never in my lifetime be as good as my Mentors. I can only be better than I was yesterday. Arrogance does not belong in Magick. Neither does measuring yourself up to another because our gifts are all different, and we merge and join and separate like the storms we create, the storms we fight, the storms we watch pass us by, the storms we help others survive.

There was a lot about J in my book, because he was a catalyst of my change. He is the love of my life, and he will always be in my life. The storm, the eye, the changes brought within. We do communicate still, we still love, we still engage. We have grown, we have battled, we have healed. Sometimes that is what we get in life and sometimes that is all we get. Pieces of of others, pieces of ourselves. Shelters in our storms that are safe. I accepted J as he was because he accepts me as I am. Satan, in all his work with me, has shown me the Eye of the Storm is a safe place, a haven of healing. It is not about being the best, having a special table or being accepted by the masses. It is about being the best version of myself. Constantly striving to be the best version of myself, constantly improving, for myself, not for anyone else's approval. Of accepting myself for who and what I am and for accepting others for who and what and where they are and not allowing others to create storms I do not want to engage in. My rise as the Eastern Star was about meeting the challenges given to me, for myself, because I was the chosen one. We are all chosen ones when asked by Satan to accomplish something. We are all special when we are asked to accomplish a goal by Satan and we are all touched by the Hand of Satan when we so choose to honor that goal.